118 Favorite Recipes From Clelia's Cucina Italiana

Clelia Graceffa Egan

Copyright © 2014 by Clelia Graceffa Egan. All rights reserved worldwide. No part of this publication may be replicated, redistributed, or given away in any form without the prior written consent of the author/publisher or the terms relayed to you herein. The contents of this book are to be used solely for educational and reference purposes.

Disclaimer: Although the information in this book is believed to be complete and accurate, errors are possible. In addition, the times given should be seen as an approximate guide because preparation times and cooking times may differ according to the techniques, equipment, and materials used by different people. This could provide a different outcome than intended. As such, the author cannot guarantee or be held responsible for what occurs in connection with the use of the information in this book.

ISBN 10: 1-50787-215-1

ISBN 13: 978-1-507-87215-4

Table of Contents

Introduction 4

About Clelia 5

About Naples 6

Starter Recipes 7

Salad Recipes 19

Pasta Recipes 29

Soup Recipes 65

Poultry Recipes 73

Beef, Veal and Pork Recipes 94

Fish Recipes 113

Vegetable/Side Dish Recipes 135

Dessert Recipes 161

Metric Conversion Chart 175

Index 176

Order book at: www.cleliascookbook.com

Introduction

118 Favorite Recipes from Clelia's Cucina Italiana is Clelia's unique collection of her own original recipes, as well as her version of popular Italian favorites, many accompanied with an appetizing full-color picture so that you will know exactly how to present your dish.

This cookbook is different from many other Italian cookbooks because:

- **Clelia was born and raised in Italy, which gives this book an authentic native influence.**

- **Many of these recipes are Clelia's own creations not found anywhere else; as well as her own versions of popular Italian recipes that everyone enjoys.**

Clelia's show, *Clelia's Cucina Italiana*, has been airing on cable television since 1995. It is one of the longest running cooking programs on television. In that time, she has taught countless fans how to cook hundreds of delicious Italian dishes like **"Stuffed Pork Tenderloin with Pancetta, Gorgonzola, and Dried Figs"** and **"Beef Braciolettine a Modo Mio"** (her way), or **"Salmon with Pignoli Nuts and Fresh Herbs"** (also her own way). This cookbook will teach you how to prepare these dishes.

Clelia will tell you the secret to cooking like an Italian. When you start creating these beautiful and delicious Italian dishes, picture yourself in a wonderful Italian village where everything is fresh out of the garden and the birds are singing, the children are playing, and somewhere you hear the sound of a wonderful song or music that Italians are known for. That should help you to create those wonderful dishes that you will find in this book.

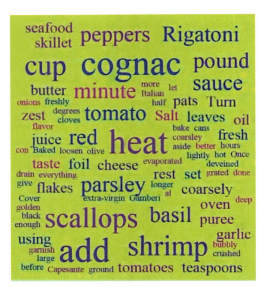

About Clelia

Clelia's interest in food and cooking started as a little girl growing up in Bagnoli, a suburb of Naples, Italy. She enjoyed helping her mother and grandmother prepare the daily meals. Around the age of nine or ten, it became her job to make ravioli for the holiday dinners for the whole family. Clelia would make over four hundred ravioli, all by hand. She liked to develop different fillings for the ravioli, much to the delight of her family.

(Mamma, questo libro e' per te!)

Growing up, she learned how to make all the typical Italian dishes, but she created her own versions of them. Clelia continues to develop many of her own delicious dishes, just by putting different ingredients, spices, and herbs together. Even at night when making the family meals, she tries to come up with new recipes trying different ingredients.

Clelia first started teaching Italian cooking at the local adult education program in 1978. Her classes were very popular and always sold out. Some of her students used to say that their families would wait at home with great anticipation to taste samples from the class. At the urging of many students, in 1995, she started *Clelia's Cucina Italiana*, an award-winning cable TV show that is still airing after twenty years. People are always stopping her to say how much they enjoy watching her show.

Among her other achievements, Clelia was a finalist in a *Good Morning America* cooking contest and had her recipe published in the *Good Morning America Cut the Calories* cookbook. She was also the winner of a Sheraton menu contest, and her recipe was put on the menu.

Clelia is passionate about her cooking and her Italian heritage. In addition to her television show, she shares her passion by teaching Italian language and culture to students eager to learn about all things Italian from someone who experienced it firsthand.

About Naples

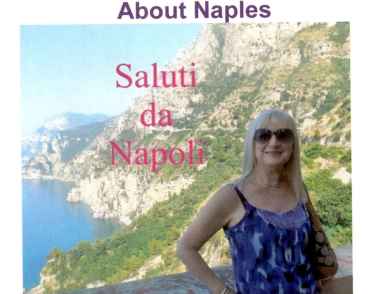

Let me tell you about Naples, my hometown. Naples is a wonderful city and I am very proud of being Napoletana. The city is beautiful, and the people are amazing. Neapolitans are basically very happy, warm, generous, loud, and excitable. Do I have enough adjectives? We are also people with a lot of faith. Our patron saint is San Gennaro, and we all pray to him for favors (la grazia). Whatever that might be or whatever we might need, we turn to San Gennaro to help us. We might be all those things and more…but most of all, we have heart. We love life. Every day is a different day. Being Napoletana is being happy. You do not have to be rich! You are just happy because you have a new baby, a new friend, a wonderful dinner with your whole family, a celebration of some kind. Maybe we are the way we are because of the Vesuvius explosion two thousand years ago. Enjoy today because tomorrow who knows (Chi lo sa!) That is what being Napoletana means!

Neapolitans are very proud of their skills, whether they are making a great pizza, creating a work of art, or some other accomplishment. Let's not forget all the beautiful music and popular songs known all over the world like "O Sole Mio," "Santa Lucia," and "Oi Mari,' all sung in the unique Neapolitan dialect, which is a language of its own. Oh, I almost forgot; Naples has the best cooks and food in the world; pizza margherita, sugo al pomodoro, the best espresso, and is also the birthplace of limoncello liqueur. We have Amalfi, Sorrento, Capri, La Grotta Azzurra, and much more. We feel that we are truly blessed with it all!

Starter Recipes

A restaurant in Florence

Roasted Tricolor Peppers Rollups

Involtini di Peperoni Rossi Arrostiti

3 peppers (red, yellow, and orange)
12 slices of prosciutto
12 slices of mild provolone cheese or smoked mozzarella cheese
1 cup of chopped basil leaves
Salt and freshly ground black pepper to taste
2 to 3 tablespoons extra-virgin olive oil

Put the peppers on a grill or under a broiler until charred on all sides. When cool enough to handle, remove the charred skins, the stems and seeds, and cut into four strips lengthwise. Place the strips on a board, blot them with some paper towels, and start assembling.

Place 1 slice of prosciutto on top of each pepper strip, top with a slice of cheese, a few pieces of basil, some salt and freshly ground black pepper, a few drops of olive oil, and fold into thirds with the cut side down. Brush with some olive oil and a little sprinkle of freshly ground black pepper. When done, place them on a cookie sheet lined with parchment paper.

Place the cookie sheet under the broiler, one rack above the middle rack for about 3 to 4 minutes or until the cheese slightly melts. Take them out of the oven, and let rest for about 2 to 3 minutes. Drizzle some olive oil on top before serving.

Yields about 12 servings.

Bruschetta

Bruschetta alla Clelia

1 loaf French bread
1 large garlic clove
1/4 cup extra-virgin olive oil
1 cup herb-flavored goat cheese or gorgonzola cheese
1/4 pound prosciutto, thinly sliced
1 small jar julienne-sliced sun-dried tomatoes in olive oil, drained
1 cup pitted kalamata olives

Slice the loaf of French bread diagonally into 1/4 to 1/2 inch slices, brush with the olive oil and toast under the broiler. Take the garlic clove, split it in half, and stab on a fork. Rub the top of the toasted slices with the garlic in order to get just the flavor from the garlic. Continue in the same manner with all the slices.

Spread the goat cheese or gorgonzola cheese on top of each slice. Top with a slice of the prosciutto folded over to fit on top of each slice of bread. Add a small piece of sun-dried tomato on top of the prosciutto, and place on a serving platter. Add the olives around the platter and serve.

Yields about 12 to 14 slices

Clelia's Antipasto

Antipasto alla Clelia

1 medium jar roasted red peppers, sliced in 1/2 inch strips
1 cup fresh basil leaves
4 to 5 marjoram sprigs, leaves only
1 medium garlic clove, minced
1/2 teaspoon salt or to taste
1/2 teaspoon freshly ground black pepper or to taste
1 cup extra-virgin olive oil

1/2 pound thinly sliced imported prosciutto
2 large balls fresh mozzarella cheese, sliced
4 large tomatoes, sliced
6 hard-boiled eggs, shelled, and cut in half or quartered
1/2 cup pitted black cured olives
1/2 cup pitted large green olives, marinated

Note: This is an antipasto, so you can add or substitute any ingredients you like. Try some marinated artichoke hearts, anchovies, provolone cheese, salami, mortadella, all good and delicious as well.

In a food processor, combine basil leaves, marjoram leaves, garlic, salt, and freshly ground black pepper, and blend to a coarse puree. With the processor still running, gradually blend in the olive oil to obtain a nice smooth blend. Transfer the herbed olive oil into a small bowl and set aside.

Arrange the prosciutto slices around the edge of a serving platter. Follow with the mozzarella slices overlapping with the tomato slices. Continue in the same manner with the pepper strips, the hard-boiled eggs, and so on, to form a nice uniform pattern. Sprinkle the olives over all, and drizzle the herbed olive oil over the antipasto. Serve with some hot crusty slices of ciabatta bread or any bread you prefer.

Serves 6 to 8 or more.

Peppers and Prosciutto Rollups

Involtini di Peperoni con Prosciutto

3 large peppers of different colors
12 ounces gorgonzola cheese or goat cheese
1/3 pound prosciutto

Cut the peppers in half and remove all the seeds and stems. Slice lengthwise into 1/4 inch strips. Place a slice of prosciutto on a wooden board and spread some of the gorgonzola or goat cheese over it. Put together a strip of each color of pepper and roll it up with the prosciutto to form a bundle. Continue in the same manner until all done.

Place on a cookie sheet lined with parchment paper and broil for about 1 minute, or just enough to seal the prosciutto around the peppers. Transfer to a serving dish and serve.

Serves 6 to 8.

Stuffed Bread with Sausage or Peppers

Mbriulata

This recipe is a family favorite. We serve it often, especially around the holidays. It makes a delicious hors d'oeuvre or something different to bring over to someone's house. I know my friends love it and always ask for it. One of my friends who tried it for the first time said, "Oh, I thought I died and went to Heaven." Sooo good!

2 store bought pizza dough, about 16 ounces each.

Sausage stuffing:

2 to 3 tablespoons extra-virgin olive oil
3 medium to large onions, thinly sliced
6 to 7 Italian sausage links, casings removed
1 cup pitted kalamata olives, whole or cut in half
Salt and freshly ground black pepper
1/2 teaspoon red pepper flakes (optional) but better

Preheat oven to 425 degrees.

In a large frying pan, add about 2 tablespoons of olive oil and the onions. Sauté the onions on medium-heat, turning often to make sure they do not burn. When the onions are translucent and a light golden color, remove from the pan and set aside to cool. In the same frying pan, add the sausage meat and start cooking, breaking it with a fork to prevent clumping together. Add some black pepper and the red pepper flakes if using. Stir the meat often just until no longer pink. Turn the heat off and set aside to cool **completely.**

At this point, sprinkle some flour on a wooden board and start rolling one of the dough balls as you would for a pizza. It does not have to be perfectly round. Roll out the dough about 1/4 inch thick or so. Spread the sausage, the onions, and the olives all over as you would on a pizza.

When done, start folding the dough away from you, almost as you would a jellyroll, making sure to keep in the stuffing. Tuck both ends under and make a couple of cuts on top with the point of a knife to let the steam escape. Brush with some olive oil all over. Very carefully, pick it up and place on a cookie sheet lined with parchment paper. Place it on the lowest rack of the oven. Cook for about 35 to 40 minutes to a nice golden color.

Allow to rest for about 20 minutes or so before slicing.

Pepper stuffing:

3 bell peppers, red, yellow, and orange, sliced into 1/2 inch strips
1 large onion, sliced
3 tablespoons extra-virgin olive oil
1 large garlic clove, thinly sliced
3 tablespoons capers rinsed, drained, and pat dried
1 cup pitted kalamata olives
1/4 cup dry breadcrumbs
Salt and freshly ground black pepper to taste

In a large frying pan, heat the olive oil on medium-high heat, and add the peppers and onions. Cook stirring often until they start to wilt slightly, but are still crunchy, about 8 to 10 minutes. Add some salt and pepper, the garlic, capers, and olives. Stir the mixture well to combine and continue to cook about 10 more minutes. Stir in the breadcrumbs, turn the heat off, and let the mixture cool **completely.**

Once the mixture is cool, sprinkle some flour on a wooden board, and roll out the dough about 1/4 inch thick or so; follow the same procedure as the sausage bread.

Allow to rest for about 20 minutes or so before slicing.

Each loaf yields 10 to 12 slices.

Polenta Panini

Panini di Polenta

Polenta:

**2 tablespoons extra-virgin olive oil
3 to 4 garlic cloves, crushed
1/2 teaspoon red pepper flakes (optional) but better
2 -1/2 cups cold water
3/4 cup polenta
2 teaspoons salt**

In a medium saucepan, heat the olive oil on medium-heat. Add the garlic cloves and sauté until lightly golden then remove. Add the water, the red pepper flakes if using, and the salt to the pan. With the heat still on medium-heat, slowly add the polenta, stirring continually until the polenta is dissolved; lower the heat to medium-low. Continue to stir the polenta until thick and creamy, about 20 to 25 minutes or so, and then turn the heat off.

Line a cookie sheet with parchment paper. Spread the polenta over the cookie sheet evenly until it is about a quarter of an inch thick or so. Let it cool completely in the refrigerator for about 25 to 30 minutes or until firm.

To make the polenta panini:

6 tablespoons extra-virgin olive oil, more if needed
2 large mozzarella balls, sliced
1/3 pound sliced prosciutto
16 to 20 basil leaves
2 to 3 eggs, beaten
1 cup seasoned breadcrumbs
Salt and freshly ground black pepper to taste

Using a cup, or a glass 2-1/2 to 3 inches in diameter turned upside down, press down onto the polenta to form a disk. Top the polenta disk with a slice of mozzarella, 2 basil leaves, and a slice of prosciutto. Top with another polenta disk in order to make a sandwich. Continue in the same manner until all done.

Heat 3 tablespoons of olive oil in a nonstick skillet on medium-high heat. Beat the eggs in a bowl with some salt and pepper to taste, and put the breadcrumbs in a flat dish. Dip the polenta sandwich first in the eggs then in the breadcrumbs. Place the sandwiches in the frying pan in batches, and cook for about 1 to 2 minutes per side, until golden and the mozzarella is just starting to melt in between. Continue in the same manner adding more olive oil if needed until all the panini are done.

Serve immediately nice and hot!

Serves 6 to 8.

Smoked Salmon and Artichoke Hearts Platter

Salmone Affumicato con Carciofi

10 to 12 ounces smoked salmon
1 (16 ounce) jar marinated artichoke hearts, drained
3 tablespoons capers in water, rinsed and drained

1/2 cup sour cream
1 tablespoon fresh dill, minced
Salt and freshly ground black pepper to taste

Arrange the salmon in a serving platter by rolling each slice and placing it around the platter in an attractive manner as shown in the picture. Add the artichokes and capers.

Mix the sour cream with the dill, salt, and freshly ground black pepper to taste. Mound it into a bowl in the middle of the platter with a little more dill sprinkled on top. Serve with some small slices of pumpernickel bread or any other bread you prefer on the side.

Serves 4 to 6.

Arancini

Arancini a Modo Mio

2 cups Arborio rice
1 small onion chopped
4 cups chicken broth
1 tablespoon extra virgin olive oil
1 pat butter
1/4 teaspoon turmeric, for color
3 egg yolks
3 whole eggs, beaten
1/2 stick butter, room temperature
1/2 cup grated Parmesan cheese
6 to 8 ounces each gorgonzola and fontina cheese cut into small cubes
1 -1/2 cups flavored breadcrumbs
Vegetable oil for frying
Tomato sauce for dipping

In a medium size saucepan, set on medium-high heat, add 1 tablespoon of olive oil and the 1 pat of butter. Add the onion and sauté until lightly golden in color, then add the rice and stir until well coated. Stir the turmeric into the chicken broth and add to the rice; cover the pan, bring to a rapid boil and then lower the heat to medium-low. Continue to cook for about 15 minutes or so stirring occasionally.

Turn the heat off, cool slightly and add the half stick of butter, the egg yolks, and the grated cheese, stirring everything well. Spread the rice onto a cookie sheet to cool **completely.**

Once the rice has cooled, start making the arancini. Take about 4 tablespoons of rice in your hand and squeeze together to form a ball. Make an indentation in the middle with your finger and insert 1 or 2 of the cheese cubes; close the ball by adding more rice if necessary, and roll again into a ball. The ball should be about the size of a small orange. Continue in the same manner alternating the cheeses until finished. Roll each ball first into the beaten eggs then in the breadcrumbs and set aside.

In a medium size saucepan about 5 inches deep, add 1-3/4 to 2 inches of vegetable oil, and heat until hot, or until a deep frying thermometer reaches between 325 to 350 F. Using a large slotted spoon, carefully lower 1 or 2 arancini at a time, into the hot oil. Cook continually turning, for about 35 to 40 seconds. When done, carefully remove each one from the pan with the slotted spoon and place in a dish lined with paper towels. Continue in the same manner until all the arancini are done.

Serve immediately nice and hot with your favorite tomato sauce, for dipping.

Yields about 8 large arancini.

Variations: Chop some pepperoni in small pieces and insert into the arancini the same way as the cheese. Also, if you like to serve them with cocktails, just make the balls as small as cocktail meatballs, and follow the same procedure with whatever filling you prefer.

Yields about 2 dozen cocktail size

Salad Recipes

Spinach Salad with Roasted Pecans

Insalata di Spinaci con Noce Pecan

2 pounds baby spinach
8 to 10 cherry tomatoes, cut in half
10 to 12 toasted pecans
Juice of one lemon

1 teaspoon Dijon mustard
1/3 cup extra-virgin olive oil
Salt and freshly ground black pepper to taste

To toast the pecans: Heat the oven to 350 degrees. Spread the pecans on a cookie sheet and place in the heated oven for about 10 to 12 minutes, stirring often. Cool before adding to salad.

Rinse the spinach in cold water and spin dry. Transfer to a salad bowl, and add the cherry tomatoes. Whisk the lemon juice, olive oil, mustard, salt and pepper. Pour the vinaigrette over the spinach just before serving. Toss well, add the toasted pecans, and serve immediately.

Serves 4 to 6.

Simple Fennel Salad

Una Semplice Insalata di Finocchio

2 fennel bulbs
1/3 cup extra-virgin olive oil
1/2 teaspoon Dijon mustard
3 tablespoons balsamic vinegar
Salt and freshly ground black pepper to taste

Cut the fern off the fennel bulbs and reserve. Cut and discard the tough outer parts of the fennel bulbs. Rinse the fennel bulbs and the fern in cold water and dry with paper towels. Cut each bulb in half and then into thin wedges. Whisk together the olive oil, vinegar, mustard, salt and pepper. Arrange the fennel wedges on a platter. Pour the dressing over them, garnish with some of the fern, and serve at once.

Serves 4 to 6.

Warm Spinach Salad with Goat Cheese

Insalata di Spinaci Tiepidi con Formaggio di Capra

2 tablespoons of extra-virgin olive oil
2 tablespoons butter
2 garlic cloves
1 medium size jar roasted red peppers cut into strips
2 large Portobello mushrooms, sliced
2 pounds baby spinach
4 to 6 ounces goat cheese
Salt and freshly ground black pepper to taste

In a medium skillet, add the olive oil and the garlic cloves. Sauté the garlic in the olive oil on medium-high heat, just until the garlic is lightly golden then discard. Add the mushrooms, the pepper strips, and salt and pepper to the same skillet. Sauté 5 to 6 minutes, on high heat, stirring often. When done, take them out of the pan, and set aside.

Add the butter and the spinach to the same skillet with some salt and pepper. Sauté just until the spinach wilts slightly. Place the spinach in a serving dish and spread it out to make a bed. Top with the mushrooms, the pepper strips, dot with the goat cheese, and serve at once.

Serves 2 to 4.

Frisee Salad

Insalata di Frisee

2 heads frisee lettuce, or the white part only of chicory lettuce
1 small red onion, thinly sliced
10 to 12 dried apricots
1 cucumber, thinly sliced
4 to 5 radishes, thinly sliced

6 to 8 whole walnuts
1/4 cup Parmesan shavings
1/3 cup extra-virgin olive oil
the juice of 1 medium pink grapefruit
Salt and freshly ground black pepper

Cut the top off the frisee lettuce or chicory. Rinse well in cold water and spin dry. Chop the frisee or chicory coarsely, and place in a salad bowl along with the red onion, the apricots, the cucumber, the radishes, and the walnuts. In a small bowl, add the olive oil, the juice of the grapefruit, and salt and pepper. Beat everything together with a fork or whisk until well combined and slightly thickened. Pour over the salad just before serving. Top with the Parmesan shavings.

Frisee is not always available, but you can replace it with the white part of the chicory, which is almost as good. Frisee and chicory both have a slightly bitter taste, but are both equally crisp and delicious!

Try them!

Simple and refreshing!

Serves 4 to 6.

Tomatoes, Basil and Mozzarella Salad

Insalata di Pomodori, Basilico, e Mozzarella

2 to 3 large mozzarella balls
4 large tomatoes about the same size as the mozzarella
20 to 25 fresh large basil leaves
1/4 cup extra-virgin olive oil (more if desired)
Salt and freshly ground black pepper

Rinse the basil well and spin dry. Rinse the tomatoes and dry with paper towels. Slice the mozzarella and the tomatoes about a quarter-inch thick. Start assembling in a serving platter by placing one slice of tomato, alternating with one basil leaf and one slice of mozzarella. Continue in the same manner until you have filled the dish. Drizzle with the olive oil, and some salt and pepper. Serve immediately.

Serves 6 to 8.

Chickpea Salad

Insalata di Ceci

2 cans ceci or chickpeas, also called (garbanzo beans), rinsed and drained
3 tender celery stalks and leaves, chopped
1 small red onion, minced
1/2 cup Italian parsley leaves, chopped
1/2 cup basil leaves, torn
4 to 6 Italian cherry hot peppers from a jar, coarsely chopped
1 garlic clove, finely minced or grated
7 to 8 tablespoons extra-virgin olive oil
2 tablespoons white balsamic vinegar
Salt and freshly ground black pepper to taste

Combine the first 7 ingredients in a large serving bowl. Whisk the olive oil, vinegar, salt and pepper together, and pour over the salad. Mix everything well and let marinate at room temperature for about one hour. Stir and garnish with more chopped parsley before serving.

Serves 6 to 8.

Fennel with Blood Oranges

Finocchio con Arance Sanguigne

2 medium-size fennel bulbs
2 blood oranges
1 organic lemon juice and zest
3 to 4 tablespoons extra-virgin olive oil
Salt and freshly ground black pepper

Cut the fern off each fennel bulb. Take off and discard the tough outer parts of the fennel. Rinse the fennel and fern and dry with paper towels. Reserve the fern. Slice the fennel in half and then into thin wedges. Peel the oranges and cut out the sections. Spread the reserved fennel fern in a serving dish to form a bed. Alternate slices of fennel and orange sections on top of the fern.

In a small bowl, add the lemon juice, lemon zest, olive oil, salt, and pepper to taste, and whisk everything well. Pour over the fennel and serve.

This salad is so delicious, quick and simple to make, that you simply must try it.

Note: If you can't find blood oranges, as they are seasonal, just use regular oranges, equally delicious.

Serves 6 to 8.

Cold Barley Salad

Insalata d'Orzo Freddo

2 cups barley
1 cup flat parsley leaves, chopped
2 sprigs of dill, finely chopped
12 cherry tomatoes cut in half
1 cup pitted kalamata olives, coarsely chopped

1/3 cup capers
5 to 6 caper berries (for garnish)
3 tablespoons white balsamic vinegar
5 to 6 tablespoons extra-virgin olive oil
Salt and plenty of freshly ground black pepper

Cook barley according to instructions on the package. Once cooked, rinse under cold water and drain well. Refrigerate overnight or for 3 to 4 hours until nice and cold. When ready to make the salad, put the barley into a serving bowl, add the first 7 ingredients and stir. Whisk together the balsamic vinegar, the oil, and salt and pepper to taste. Pour over the salad and leave to marinate in the refrigerator until you are ready to serve.

Serves 6 to 8.

Orange and Arugula Salad

Isalata di Arancia e Arugula

4 oranges
1 bunch large arugula leaves (not baby arugula))
15 black cured olives or kalamata olives, pitted
3 tablespoons balsamic vinegar, good Italian brand
1/3 cup extra virgin olive oil
Salt and freshly ground black pepper to taste

Rinse the arugula in cold water and spin dry. Peel the oranges and slice them about one quarter inch thick. Place on a serving platter, alternating orange slices and arugula leaves all around the dish as shown in the picture. Scatter some olives on top. Beat together the vinegar, olive oil, salt and pepper, just until it slightly thickens. Add to the salad just before serving.

Very tasty and refreshing!

Serves 4 to 6.

Pasta Recipes

Pappardelle with Bolognese Sauce

Pappardelle alla Bolognese

1 pound pappardelle pasta
1 small to medium onion, chopped
2 garlic cloves, minced
3 tablespoons extra virgin olive oil, more if needed
1 cup celery, chopped small
1 cup carrots, chopped small
2 sprigs of basil, leaves only, torn
1/2 pound each of ground beef, pork, and veal
2 ((28 ounce) cans crushed tomatoes
2 tablespoons tomato paste
3/4 cup dry red wine, good Italian brand
1/2 cup grated Parmesan cheese
Salt and freshly ground black pepper

Heat a large skillet on medium-high heat and add the olive oil and the onion. Cook until the onion is slightly soft. Turn the heat down to medium, add the garlic, celery, and carrots, and continue to cook stirring often, until all the vegetables are soft, about 5 to 6 minutes or so.

Return the heat up to medium-high, and add the meat. Cook and stir until the meat is no longer pink and there are no meat clumps. Add the tomatoes, tomato paste, wine, basil, and salt and pepper to taste. Turn the heat down to medium-low and continue to cook the sauce for about 1 hour or so uncovered, stirring occasionally.

Cook the pappardelle pasta according to package directions. When done, drain the pappardelle and transfer to a serving bowl. Add about two ladles of sauce and stir the pappardelle gently. Top with more sauce, a good sprinkle of Parmesan cheese, and serve immediately with more sauce and cheese to pass around at the table. Delicious!

Serves 4 to 6.

Rotini with Pesto Mediterraneo

Rotini con Pesto Mediterraneo

1 pound rotini pasta
2 -1/2 cups basil leaves
1/3 cup parsley leaves
1/3 cup celery (white tender part only)
1 cup baby arugula
Salt and pepper to taste

2 small garlic cloves, chopped
1/2 cup pignoli (pine nuts, or slivered almonds)
1/2 cup extra-virgin olive oil
3 medium tomatoes
1/2 cup grated Pecorino Romano cheese

Put about 1 quart of water in a medium pan and bring to a boil. Drop in the tomatoes for about 40 seconds. Run them under cold water to cool. Peel, seed and chop the tomatoes, and set aside.

In a food processor, process the garlic and pine nuts or almonds; add the basil, celery, parsley, arugula, salt, and freshly ground black pepper to taste. Continue to process adding the olive oil while the processor is running. Add more olive oil if needed. Do not process too long as the mixture should be slightly coarse.

Pour the mixture into a bowl. Stir in the chopped tomatoes and about 1/3 cup of the cheese. Gently mix everything well, and set aside.

Cook the rotini according to package directions. Save about 1/4 cup of pasta water before draining, then put the pasta back in the same pan. Add the pesto and the pasta water and gently stir everything together. Transfer to a serving bowl, sprinkle the top with the remaining cheese, and a drizzle of olive oil, and serve.

Serves 4 to 6.

Pasta Carbonara

Pasta alla Carbonara

1 pound spaghetti or linguini
2 tablespoons extra-virgin olive oil
6 ounces pancetta, coarsely chopped
Salt and pepper to taste

1 egg and 3 egg yolks
1/3 cup medium cream
1/2 cup Parmesan cheese (have more to sprinkle and pass around)

Heat the olive oil in a frying pan on medium-high heat. Add the chopped pancetta and sauté until the pancetta is crispy but not burned. Turn the heat off and set aside.

In the meantime, cook pasta according to package directions.

In a medium bowl, add the egg, the yolks, cheese, cream, and salt and pepper to taste. Beat everything together and set aside. When the pasta is cooked, drain it and put it back in the same pan. Stir in the cream mixture and some pancetta and mix well. Pour the pasta into a serving bowl and sprinkle with more cheese. Garnish with the rest of the pancetta and serve at once.

Very tasty and easy!

Serves 4 to 6.

Penne with Red and Yellow Peppers

Penne con Peperoni Rossi e Gialli

1 pound penne pasta
1 each, red and yellow bell pepper, sliced into thin, short strips
2 tablespoons capers, rinsed in cold water and drained
1 medium clove garlic, minced
2 anchovy filets, minced
6 tablespoons extra-virgin olive oil,

1/2 pound mozzarella bites (bocconcini)
Parmesan cheese for sprinkling
20 to 25 basil leaves, coarsly chopped, save some whole for garnish
Salt and freshly ground black pepper to taste

Heat 2 tablespoons of olive oil in a skillet and start to sauté the peppers on medium-high heat. Stir-fry the peppers for about 10 minutes, stirring often to keep them nice and crunchy. When done, turn the heat off, and leave them in the skillet.

In the meantime, put the garlic, chopped basil, anchovies, capers and 2 tablespoons of olive oil in a food processor. Process until well blended, then add to the skillet with the peppers. Stir in 1 more tablespoon of olive oil, some salt and freshly ground black pepper to taste. Mix everything together well and set aside.

Cook pasta according to package directions. When the pasta is cooked, take out about 1/4 cup of the pasta water before draining. Put the pasta back in the same pan. Stir in the pasta water, the pepper mixture, and the mozzarella bites.

Gently mix everything well. Pour it all in a serving bowl; add a drizzle of olive oil and some grated Parmesan cheese. Garnish with some of the whole-leaf basil, and serve at once with more Parmesan cheese to pass around at the table.

Serves 4 to 6.

Ziti with Herbs and Gorgonzola Cheese

Ziti con Erbe e Gorgonzola

1 pound ziti pasta
2 pounds tomatoes, coarsely chopped
1 cup scallions, white and light green part, chopped
2 small sprigs of fresh dill, coarsely chopped
1 cup fresh flat parsley leaves, coarsely chopped
1/2 cup fresh marjoram leaves, coarsley chopped

1/2 cup fresh basil leaves, coarsely chopped
8 to 10 ounces of gorgonzola cheese, coarsely chopped
1/2 cup extra-virgin olive oil
1 to 2 teaspoons freshly ground black pepper or to taste
1/2 teaspoon salt or to taste

In a bowl, mix together the tomatoes, scallions, dill, parsley, marjoram, basil, olive oil, salt and pepper, and set aside.

Cook ziti according to package directions. When the pasta is cooked, take out about 1/2 cup of the pasta water before draining. Once the pasta is drained, put it back in the same pan. Add the cheese while the pasta is still hot. Stir gently until the cheese starts to slightly melt.

Add all the other ingredients from the bowl and some of the pasta water to make it moist. Mix everything well, transfer to a serving bowl, and serve at once.

Serves 4 to 6.

Pasta with Salted Ricotta

Pasta con Ricotta Salata

1 pound spaghetti or linguini
3 tablespoons extra-virgin olive oil
2 garlic cloves, sliced
1 (7-ounce) jar julienne sun-dried tomatoes, drained
2 pounds cherry tomatoes, cut in half or in quarters, if large
1/3 cup pignoli nuts (pine nuts)
1 bunch fresh basil (25 leaves or so), rinsed and spun-dried
1/2 cup grated Pecorino Romano or Parmesan cheese
3 tablespoons ricotta salata shavings (shave with vegetable peeler)
Salt and black pepper to taste

Start by making the sauce first.

Heat a skillet on medium-heat with 3 tablespoons of extra-virgin olive oil. Add the garlic and sauté until lightly golden. Add the drained sun-dried tomatoes and sauté for about 2 minutes longer. Put in the cherry tomatoes, pine nuts, basil leaves, salt, and freshly ground black pepper to taste, and mix everything well.

Continue to cook uncovered on medium-low heat. Mash the tomatoes slightly with the back of a spoon or potato masher to speed up the cooking. Stir often to prevent sticking.

Cook the pasta according to package directions. When the pasta is ready, drain it and pour it in a serving bowl. Add the sauce, the grated cheese, and some of the ricotta salata shavings. Mix everything well. Garnish with the remaining ricotta salata shavings and basil leaves and serve immediately.

Serves 4 to 6.

Shells with Ricotta and Mozzarella

Conchiglie con Ricotta e Mozzarella

1 pound medium-size shells
16 ounces ricotta
8 ounces shredded mozzarella
1/2 cup grated Pecorino Romano

Marinara Sauce:

2 (28-ounce) cans of chunky or crushed tomatoes (good Italian brand)
1 tablespoon tomato paste
3 tablespoons extra-virgin olive oil
4 large garlic cloves, crushed
About 15 to 20 fresh basil leaves
1/4 teaspoon red pepper flakes (optional)
Salt and freshly ground black pepper to taste

In a medium saucepan, heat the olive oil on medium-high heat and add the garlic. Sauté until the garlic is a light golden color. Add the red pepper flakes if using, the tomatoes, the tomato paste, some of the basil leaves, and salt and pepper to taste. Lower the heat to medium-low, and cook uncovered for about 35 to 45 minutes stirring occasionally.

Cook the shells according to package directions. When the pasta is cooked, drain it and put it back in the same pan. Keep the heat on simmer and immediately add about 2 or 3 ladles of the tomato sauce, a sprinkle of Romano cheese, and the ricotta. Stir until everything is well combined. Add the mozzarella, another ladle of sauce, and stir quickly just until the mozzarella starts to slightly melt.

Transfer to a serving bowl, add a little more sauce on top, and another sprinkle of Romano cheese. Garnish with some basil leaves, and serve immediately.

Serves 4 to 6.

Spaghetti with Garlic and Olive Oil

Pasta Aglio e Olio

1 pound spaghetti
1/2 cup extra-virgin olive oil
2 pats of butter
4 garlic cloves, thinly sliced
1/4 teaspoon red pepper flakes
2 to 3 anchovy filets
1/2 cup Romano cheese
1 cup Italian parsley leaves, coarsely chopped

Cook pasta according to package directions.

While the pasta is cooking, heat a frying pan on medium-high heat and add about 1/4 cup of the olive oil and the 2 pats of butter, Add the garlic and the red pepper flakes, stirring quickly so as not to burn the garlic, about 25 to 30 seconds. Add the anchovy filets and continue to stir until the anchovies are completely dissolved, then turn the heat off.

Once the pasta is cooked, take out about half a cup of the pasta water and set aside. Drain the pasta and put it back in the same pan. Quickly add the garlic sauce, some of the pasta water, the remaining olive oil, the parsley, and a good sprinkle of cheese. Mix everything well and transfer to a serving bowl. Stir and serve immediately with more cheese to pass around at the table.

This recipe is quick to make and a favorite for Italians as a late night cena.

Serves 4 to 6.

Stuffed Shells

Conchiglie Ripiene

Marinara Sauce:

3 (28-ounce) cans chunky or crushed tomatoes (good Italian brand)
2 tablespoons tomato paste
3 tablespoons extra-virgin olive oil
5 large garlic cloves, crushed
1 cup fresh basil (leaves only)
1/4 teaspoon red pepper flakes
Salt and freshly ground black pepper to taste

Heat the olive oil in a saucepan on medium-high heat and add the garlic. Sauté until lightly golden, then add the red pepper flakes, the tomatoes, the tomato paste, and salt and pepper. Stir and lower the heat to medium-low. Cook uncovered for about 1 hour or so, stirring occasionally. Add half of the basil during the last 5 minutes of the cooking time.

Preheat the oven to 350 degrees.

1 pound giant shell pasta
2 pounds whole ricotta
1/3 pound good-quality ground beef
1/2 cup shredded mozzarella
1/2 cup freshly grated Parmesan cheese (grate more for serving)
Salt and pepper to taste

Mix the ricotta, beef, mozzarella, Parmesan cheese, salt and pepper, and some chopped basil leaves. Mix all the ingredients well and set aside.

Cook the pasta for about 8 to 9 minutes, not fully cooked. Drain and place in a bowl. Gently stir 1 tablespoon or so of olive oil to prevent shells from sticking together. When cool enough to handle, stuff the ricotta mixture into each shell with a teaspoon.

In a large roasting pan, add about 3 ladles of the tomato sauce; enough to cover the bottom of the pan. Add all the stuffed shells in a single layer and top with 3 to 4 more ladles of sauce. Cover with foil, and place in the hot oven. Cook for about 45 minutes or so.

Take the foil off for the last 15 minutes of the cooking time. When done, remove the pan from the oven, and let rest loosely covered, for 10 to 15 minutes before serving. Garnish with some more basil and serve. Pass around more sauce and Parmesan cheese at the table, if you like.

Great for a Sunday dinner!

Serves 6 to 8.

Rotini with Chicken, Asparagus, and Sour Cream

Rotini con Pollo, Asparagi e Crema Acida

1 pound rotini
4 tablespoons extra virgin olive oil
4 pats of butter
1 medium to large onion, chopped
2 large garlic cloves, chopped
1 pound thin asparagus, cut diagonally
Salt and pepper to taste

1-1/2 pounds chicken tenders, cut into bite size
1/4 cup flour for dusting
3 large Portobello mushrooms, sliced
1/2 teaspoon lemon pepper
1 (16-ounce) container sour cream
1 tablespoon Dijon mustard
1/3 cup grated Parmesan or Romano cheese

Heat 2 tablespoons of olive oil and 2 pats of butter in a large frying pan on medium-high heat. Sprinkle the chicken with some salt and pepper; dust it with some flour, and add to the frying pan. Sauté to a light golden color, about 8 to 9 minutes, stirring often. When done, remove from the pan, cover, and set aside.

In the same frying pan, add the onion and garlic and a little more olive oil if needed. Continue to sauté until the onion and garlic become soft and light golden in color. Add the asparagus and continue to sauté, stirring everything for about 2 more minutes. Remove from the pan and add to the chicken. Cover and set aside.

In the same frying pan, heat the remaining olive oil and butter. Turn the heat on high; add the mushrooms, and continue to cook and stir for about 5 to 6 minutes longer.

At this point, add the chicken and the asparagus to the mushrooms, sprinkle with the lemon pepper, and stir in the sour cream and mustard. Cover and simmer for about 2 minutes, stirring once. Turn the heat off while you cook the pasta.

Cook the rotini according to the package directions. When the pasta is cooked, take out about 1/4 cup of the pasta water, before draining and keep aside. Drain the pasta and put it back in the same pan. Add the chicken and vegetable mixture to the pasta and gently stir everything well. Stir in the pasta water a little bit at a time until you get a soft creamy sauce. Continue to simmer just until heated through. Transfer to a serving dish and sprinkle the top with some grated cheese.

Serve at once with more grated cheese to pass around at the table if you like.

Serves 4 to 6.

Pasta with Shellfish in a Gorgonzola Sauce

Pasta con Frutta di Mare alla Salsa di Gorgonzola

- 1 pound rigatoni or penne
- 2 tablespoons extra-virgin olive oil
- 4 pats butter
- 1 small onion, chopped
- 1 tablespoon flour
- 1 pound shrimp, shelled and deveined
- 1 pound scallops
- 2 cups light cream
- 2 tablespoons white wine
- 6 ounces gorgonzola cheese
- 5 to 6 slices smoked salmon, coarsely chopped
- Parmesan cheese for sprinkling
- Some chopped parsley for garnish
- Salt and freshly ground black pepper to taste

Heat a large skillet on medium-high heat and add 1 tablespoon of olive oil and 1 pat of butter. Sprinkle the scallops and shrimp with salt and pepper. Add the scallops to the skillet and sauté for about 2 minutes; add the shrimp and sauté just until the shrimp turns pink, about 1 more minute or so. Take the seafood out of the skillet, place in a dish and set aside.

In the same skillet, heat 2 more pats of butter and 1 tablespoon of extra virgin olive oil over medium-high heat. Add the chopped onion and sauté until translucent and lightly golden, about 2 to 3 minutes. Remove from the skillet and add to the seafood. Put 1 more pat of butter and the flour in the same skillet. Stir continually until well blended and thickend in order to form a roux. Stir in the white wine and cook and stir for about 2 minutes longer until the wine evaporates. Add the 2 cups of cream, salt, and freshly ground black pepper.

Continue to stir and cook until the sauce thickens to a smooth consistency, about 2 minutes. Add the gorgonzola cheese and continue to stir and cook until the cheese has melted and you have a nice creamy sauce. At this point, add the seafood and onion back to the same skillet; turn the heat off, and set aside while you cook the pasta.

Cook the pasta according to package directions. Once the pasta is cooked, drain it, and put it back in the same pan. Add in the sauce with the seafood and gently simmer until everything is heated through, and all the flavors are well blended together. Transfer to a serving dish; gently stir in the chopped salmon, and a sprinkle of Parmesan cheese. Garnish with some parsley, and serve at once.

Serves 6 to 8.

Rotini with Fresh Vegetables and Goat Cheese

Rotini con Verdure e Formaggio di Capra

1 pound rotini pasta
1 cup shredded carrots
1 bunch thin asparagus, cut diagonally
6 large white mushrooms, sliced
2 large garlic cloves, minced
1 onion, chopped
6 to 8 ounces goat cheese
Salt and pepper to taste
4 tablespoons extra-virgin olive oil
3 pats of butter
10 to 12 basil leaves, coarsely chopped
4 to 5 sprigs Italian parsley leaves, coarsely chopped
Parmesan cheese for sprinkling

Heat a large frying pan on medium-high heat, and add about 3 tablespoons of extra virgin olive oil and the 3 pats of butter. Add the onion, and cook just until soft; add the carrots and the asparagus and continue to sauté for about 2 more minutes. Add the garlic and the mushrooms, some salt and pepper to taste, and continue to cook still on high heat, stirring until all the vegetables are cooked but still crunchy. Turn the heat off, and set aside.

Cook the pasta according to package directions. When the pasta is cooked, take out about 1/4 cup of the pasta water before draining it. Once drained, put the pasta back in the same pan, toss in the vegetables and stir in the goat cheese, basil, parsley, and the pasta water. Adjust the seasoning if needed, stir everything gently, and simmer just until everything is heated through.

Transfer to a serving dish, drizzle the pasta with about 1 more tablespoon of olive oil, and a sprinkle of Parmesan cheese.

Serve at once.

Serves 4 to 6.

Orzo Pasta with Asparagus

Orzo Pasta con Asparagi

**2 cups orzo pasta
1 package thin asparagus, cut about 1 to 2 inches long
2 tablespoons extra-virgin olive oil
3 pats of butter
1 medium onion, chopped
6 to 8 cups chicken broth
Salt and freshly ground black pepper to taste**

In a medium size pan add 1 tablespoon of extra-virgin olive oil and 2 pats of butter. Set the heat on medium-high and add the chopped onion. Sauté the onion until translucent and light golden in color. Add the orzo pasta and stir until well coated with the olive oil and butter. Add about 6 cups of chicken broth, stir, cover the pan, and turn the heat down to medium. As soon as the pan starts to boil, lower the heat to medium-low, stir and continue to cook covered for about 8 to 10 minutes adding more broth if necessary, so that the pasta will be nice and creamy and not dry.

While the pasta is cooking, heat a skillet on medium-high heat and add about 1 tablespoon of olive oil and 1 pat of butter. Add the asparagus, salt and pepper to taste and sauté stirring often. Cook for about 5 to 6 minutes until the asparagus are just tender. Add the asparagus to the pasta, adjust the seasoning if needed, and cook with the pasta for 1 more minute in order to blend in the flavors. Transfer the pasta to a serving dish and serve at once.

Serves 4 to 6 as a side dish.

Baked Rigatoni with Seafood and Cognac

Rigatoni al Forno con Gamberi Capesante e Cognac

1 pound rigatoni pasta
3 tablespoons extra-virgin olive oil
2 pats butter
1 each red and yellow, pepper, coarsely chopped
1 medium onion, chopped
3 garlic cloves, chopped
1/2 teaspoon red pepper flakes (optional but better)
3 (28-ounce) cans of crushed tomatoes
2 tablespoons tomato paste
20 to 25 fresh basil leaves, coarsely chopped
1/2 cup Italian parsley leaves, coarsely chopped
1 organic lemon, (use only 2 teaspoons of the juice and 2 teaspoons of the zest)
Salt and freshly ground black pepper to taste
1 pound scallops
1 pound shrimp, shelled and deveined
1/4 cup cognac
1/2 cup grated Parmesan cheese for sprinkling

Preheat the oven to 400 degrees.

Heat the olive oil in a large deep skillet on medium-high heat. Add the onion, garlic, and the peppers. Cook just until the onions and the peppers are soft and lightly golden. Add the tomatoes, the tomato paste, red pepper flakes if using, and salt and pepper to taste. Stir and cook uncovered on medium-low heat for about 1 hour or so, stirring occasionally. When done, cover and leave on the stove.

While the sauce is cooking, in a medium skillet set on medium-high heat, add the pats of butter and the scallops and sauté for about 1 minute; add the shrimp, and continue to sauté for 1 minute longer, just until the shrimp turns pink; add the lemon juice, zest, and the cognac. Continue to cook for another minute or so just until the cognac evaporates. Turn the heat off, and set aside.

Cook pasta according to package directions. When cooked, drain it, and pour it in a 9 x 13 roasting pan, or a large roasting pan.

Add the seafood to the tomato sauce, stir, and add everything to the pasta. Stir in the basil and parsely reserving some for garnish. Cover with foil, and bake for about 10 to 15 minutes or so until hot and bubbly. When done, take it out of the oven, loosen the foil, and let it rest for about 15 minutes or so. Garnish with the reserved basil and parsley, and serve at once.

Delicious!

Serves 6 to 8.

Bow Tie Pasta with Portobello Mushrooms

Farfalle con Funghi Portobello

1 pound bow tie pasta
6 to 7 medium sized Portobello mushrooms, sliced
2 tablespoons extra-virgin olive oil
2 tablespoons butter
3 medium shallots, minced
3 medium garlic cloves, minced
1/2 cup chunky or crushed tomatoes (good Italian brand)
2 tablespoons tomato paste
1/3 cup sun-dried tomatoes in olive oil, drained and chopped
1/2 cup dry red wine
1/4 cup beef broth
1/4 cup pignoli nuts, toasted*
2 sprigs thyme, leaves only
2 sprigs Italian parsley, leaves only
Salt and freshly ground black pepper to taste
Parmesan or Romano cheese for sprinkling

*To toast pignoli: Put pignoli nuts in a small skillet on medium-low heat and shake skillet back and forth for about 25 seconds or until pignoli are light golden in color. Be careful because they burn quickly!

Heat the olive oil and butter in a large frying pan on medium-heat. Add the shallots and sauté lightly until soft and then add the garlic and the mushrooms. Continue to cook and stir for about 5 to 7 minutes longer. Add the tomatoes, the tomato paste, the sun-dried tomatoes, and stir.

Cook for about 8 to 10 more minutes; add the wine, beef broth, thyme, and parsley. Continue to cook everything for about 20 to 25 minutes longer on medium-low heat, uncovered. When done, stir in the pignoli nuts, a little more freshly ground black pepper to taste, turn the heat off, cover and keep warm.

Cook pasta according to package directions. When the pasta is cooked, reserve about 1/4 cup of the pasta water before draining, then put it back into the same pan. Stir in the pasta water and add 1 to 2 ladles of the sauce, mix everything well and transfer to a serving dish. Arrange some more of the mushroom sauce on top of the pasta and a sprinkle of cheese for a nice presentation.

Serve at once.

Serves 4 to 6.

Spaghetti with Pesto Genovese

Spaghetti al Pesto Genovese

1 pound spaghetti pasta
2 cups basil leaves (packed)
1/3 cup pignoli nuts
1 garlic clove, minced*
1/2 cup Pecorino cheese, freshly grated
1/2 cup Parmesan cheese, freshly grated
1 cup extra-virgin olive oil (more if needed)

Cook spaghetti according to package directions. While the pasta is cooking, start making the pesto. In a food processor, add the basil and process for a few seconds, just enough to get the basil chopped. Add the garlic, and the pine nuts and continue to process, adding the olive oil while the processor is going. Process the pesto to a smooth consistency. When done, stir in the Pecorino and the Parmesan cheese until it is all well combined. Pour the pesto into a bowl and set aside.

Once the pasta is cooked, take out about 1/4 cup of pasta water before draining. Put the pasta back in the pan, add the pasta water to the pesto sauce a few tablespoons at a time and stir it well to make a smooth sauce. Add to the spaghetti and toss all again. Transfer the pasta to a serving dish; sprinkle a little cheese on top, and serve immediately, passing more cheese around at the table.

Serves 4 to 6.

* If you do not like raw garlic, just Sauté the garlic clove in a small skillet with 1 tablespoon of olive oil on medium-low heat, just until golden in color, and add and process with the rest of the ingredients according to the instructions.

Vegetable Lasagna

Lasagne con Verdure

1 pound lasagna pasta
1 broccoli, cut up in small florets
1 each, red pepper, yellow pepper, and orange pepper, sliced
1 medium zucchini, sliced
1 yellow squash, sliced
3 large Portobello mushrooms, sliced (gills removed if you like)

2 pounds ricotta cheese
6 eggs
3 large mozzarella balls
1 cup freshly grated Parmesan cheese (Reggiano preferably)
7 to 8 tablespoons extra-virgin olive oil

Start by making the tomato sauce first.

3 (28-ounce) cans chunky or crushed tomatoes (good Italian brand)
2 tablespoons tomato paste
4 garlic cloves, crushed
1/4 teaspoon red pepper flakes (optional)

2 tablespoons extra-virgin olive oil
12 fresh basil leaves
Salt and freshly ground black pepper to taste

Heat 2 tablespoons of olive oil in a saucepan. Add the garlic and sauté just until light golden in color; add the red pepper flakes if using, the tomatoes, and the tomato paste. Stir and cook on medium-high heat just until it starts bubbling. Then lower the heat to medium-low; add some of the basil leaves, and some salt and freshly ground black pepper. Cook uncovered for about 1 hour or so, stirring occasionally.

In the meantime, rinse the vegetables and dry them well with paper towels. Cut the peppers in half, discard the seeds and pith, and use only half of each pepper, save the rest for another use. Cut the peppers into small strips, then slice the zucchini, the yellow squash, and the mozzarella into 1/4-inch slices. Combine the ricotta, eggs, salt, and pepper; beat together well and set aside.

In a large frying pan, heat about 3 tablespoons of olive oil on high-heat and add the peppers, salt and pepper to taste; sauté stirring often for about 2 to 3 minutes. Add the zucchini, the yellow squash, the broccoli florets, and the mushrooms. Continue to sauté, still on high-heat, stirring often for about 2 to 3 minutes longer. Turn heat off, and set aside.

Preheat oven to 375 degrees.

At this point, start cooking the lasagna according to package directions. When the lasagna is cooked, drain, transfer to a large dish; gently mix in 1 tablespoon of olive oil to prevent lasagna from sticking together and set aside.

In an 11 x 13 roasting pan, put in about 2 ladles of the tomato sauce, enough to cover the bottom of the pan. Spread 3 to 4 pieces of the lasagna noodles, top with some of the ricotta mixture, some of the vegetables and mozzarella slices, a good sprinkle of Parmesan cheese, and about 1 more ladle of tomato sauce. Continue to layer in the same manner, starting again with the lasagna noodles, ricotta, vegetables, mozzarella, Parmesan cheese, and sauce. End the top layer with more tomato sauce, mozzarella slices, and a good sprinkle of Parmesan cheese.

Cover loosely with foil; do not seal. Bake for about 30 to 35 minutes. When done, take the pan out of the oven, and let it rest for about 15 minutes or so before serving. Pass more sauce and cheese at the table if you like.

Serves 8 to 10.

Clelia's Classic Lasagna

Lasagne alla Clelia

Start by making the tomato sauce first:

4 to 5 baby back pork ribs to flavor the sauce
4 to 5 large garlic cloves, crushed
2 tablespoons extra virgin olive oil
3 (28-ounce) cans of crushed tomatoes
2 tablespoons tomato paste
1 cup fresh basil leaves, torn
1/4 teaspoon red pepper flakes
Salt and freshly ground black pepper to taste

Heat the olive oil in a large saucepan on medium-high heat. Sprinkle the ribs with salt and pepper to taste, and Sauté stirring and turning until golden all over. Add the garlic and continue to Sauté just until golden. Add the tomatoes, the tomato paste, half of the basil, and the red pepper flakes. Stir until everything is well incorporated, and continue to cook on medium-high just until the sauce starts to slightly bubble. Lower the heat to medium-low, and cook uncovered for about 1 hour or so.

When done, taste, stir in the rest of the basil, adjust the seasoning if needed, cover, and leave on the stove while you prepare the lasagna.

1 pound lasagna pasta
1 pound lean ground beef
1/2 pound lean ground pork
1 (32-ounce) container whole milk ricotta
4 large fresh mozzarella balls

6 extra large eggs
1 cup grated Parmesan cheese, more to sprinkle
2 tablespoons extra virgin olive oil
Salt and freshly ground black pepper to taste

Preheat the oven to 350 degrees.

Heat a non-stick skillet on medium-high heat and add 1 tablespoon of olive oil. When the olive oil is hot, add the ground beef and the pork and a sprinkle of salt and pepper to taste. Continue to cook and stir, breaking the meat with a fork so that it will not clump together. Sauté until the meat is no longer pink. Turn the heat off; drain any fat left in the skillet, and set aside.

Cook the lasagna according to the package directions. In a large bowl, mix together the ricotta, the eggs, and salt and pepper to taste. Slice the mozzarella into thin slices. When the pasta is cooked, drain it, and drizzle about 1 tablespoon of olive oil so that the pasta won't stick together. Spread on a cookie sheet to cool. When cool enough to handle, start assembling the lasagna.

In a 10 x 13 roasting pan or a large roasting pan, add about a laddle or two of the tomato sauce; enough to cover the bottom of the pan, top with a layer of lasagna noodles, enough to cover the bottom of the pan as well, then spread over it some of the ricotta mixture, some ground meat, some slices of mozzarella, a generous sprinkle of Parmesan cheese and more sauce. Continue in the same manner until you reach the top of the pan. End the top layer with the lasagna noodles, mozzarella, sauce, and a good sprinkle of Parmesan cheese.

Cover loosely with foil. Place in the heated oven and cook for about 55 to 60 minutes or so. Remove the foil the last 10 to 15 minutes of the cooking time.

Take the pan out of the oven, cover loosely with foil and let rest for about 15 to 20 minutes before serving.

Have a feast!

Serves 8 to 12.

Shells with Broccoli Rabe and Sausage

Conchiglie con Broccoli Rape e Salsicce

**1 pound shells pasta or other short pasta
6 Italian sweet sausage links
3 tablespoons extra virgin olive oil
2 bunches broccoli rabe
4 garlic cloves, crushed
1/2 teaspoon red pepper flakes or to taste (optional but better)
Salt and freshly ground black pepper to taste
Grated Romano cheese to sprinkle and pass around at the table**

Remove and discard the tough outer leaves of the broccoli rabe, leaving the tender leaves and the florets. Peel the outer layer of the stems with a vegetable peeler in order to make the stems more tender. Rinse in cold water to remove any sand, and strain in a colander or even better a salad spinner, then roughly chop them and set aside.

Heat 1 tablespoon of olive oil in a large frying pan on medium-heat, and add the sausages. Cook the sausages until golden all over and cooked through. When done, remove the sausages from the pan onto a plate; cover and keep warm.

In the same frying pan, with the heat still on medium, add 2 tablespoons of olive oil, and the garlic cloves, Sauté until lightly golden in color, then add the red pepper flakes, all the broccoli rabe, a sprinkle of salt and stir. Cover and cook for about 3 to 5 minutes until the broccoli rabe wilts down, stirring a few times.

When the broccoli rabe has wilted down, take the cover off, stir, and continue cooking for about 5 to 6 minutes longer or until the broccoli rabe is tender. Slice the sausages into bite size and add to the broccoli rabe. Sauté everything together for about 5 to 6 more minutes to blend the flavors. Adjust the seasoning if needed, turn the heat off, cover and keep warm while you cook the pasta.

Cook pasta according to package directions. When the pasta is cooked, reserve 1/4 cup of the pasta water before draining. Return the pasta back to the same pan, turn the heat to simmer, add the broccoli rabe and sausage, and the reserved pasta water. Give it a good stir, and continue to simmer until it all blends well together and everything is heated through. Transfer to a serving bowl; drizzle with a little more olive oil, a sprinkle of Romano cheese and serve.

One of my favorites!

Serves 4 to 6.

Ziti with Mushrooms and Artichokes
Ziti con Funghi e Carciofi

1 pound ziti pasta
4 to 5 tablespoons extra virgin olive oil
3 pats of butter
6 Portobello mushrooms, sliced
1 package frozen artichoke hearts (defrosted and pat dried)
2 large garlic cloves, sliced
1 tablespoon flour
1/2 cup chicken broth
1 sprig each, Italian parsley, thyme, and oregano leaves, chopped
Salt and freshly ground black pepper
1/3 cup grated Parmesan or Pecorino Romano cheese, plus more for sprinkling

Heat a large skillet on medium-high heat. Add 1 tablespoon of olive oil and 2 pats of butter. When the butter has melted, add the artichokes, salt, and pepper to taste. Cover and cook for about 5 minutes or so, stirring once until the artichokes become soft. Take the cover off, lower the heat to medium, and add the other pat of butter, the garlic, and the mushrooms. Stir and continue to cook uncovered for about 6 to 8 minutes longer, until everything has cooked through. Transfer to a dish and set aside.

Heat the same skillet on medium-high heat. In a bowl, add 1/2 cup of chicken broth and 1 tablespoon of flour. Stir together well to dissolve the flour and then add to the skillet along with the grated cheese. Continue to cook and stir until the sauce slightly thickens and blends well with the cheese, about 5 to 6 minutes longer. Turn the heat off and set aside.

Cook pasta according to package directions. When the pasta is cooked, take out about 1/4 cup of the pasta water before draining. Once drained, put the pasta back in the same pan, turn the heat to simmer, add the artichoke and mushroom mixture, the herbs, some of the pasta water if needed, a good drizzle of olive oil, some freshly ground black pepper to taste, and continue to cook just until everything has heated through.

Transfer to a serving bowl; drizzle with a little more olive oil on top, a sprinkle of cheese, and some freshly ground black pepper.

Serve immediately with more grated cheese to pass around at the table if you like.

Serves 4 to 6.

Pasta Puttanesca

Pasta alla Puttanesca

1 pound linguini or spaghetti
3 tablespoons extra-virgin olive oil
4 garlic cloves, crushed
2 (28-ounce) cans chunky or crushed tomatoes (good Italian brand)
1 tablespoon tomato paste
3 tablespoons capers, rinsed in cold water and drained
1 can anchovy filets in olive oil, drained, (use only 4 anchovies)
1/2 cup pitted kalamata olives
1/2 cup Italian parsley leaves, coarsely chopped
1 cup basil leaves, coarsely chopped
1/4 cup oregano leaves, coarsely chopped
1/2 cup freshly grated Parmesan cheese (preferably Reggiano) more for sprinkling
1/4 teaspoon hot red pepper flakes
Salt and freshly ground black pepper

In a large frying pan, heat the olive oil to medium-high heat, then add the garlic cloves, and the anchovies. Sauté and stir until the garlic takes a light golden color, and the anchovies have just about melted, about 30 to 35 seconds. Add the tomatoes, the tomato paste, capers, olives, basil, parsley, oregano, red pepper flakes, and a sprinkle of salt and black pepper. Lower the heat to medium-low and cook for about 45 to 50 minutes uncovered, stirring occasionally.

Cook the pasta according to package directions. When the pasta is cooked, drain it and put it back in the same pan. Add about 2 ladles of the tomato sauce and stir well. Transfer to a serving bowl and top with more of that delicious tomato sauce, a good sprinkle of the Parmesan cheese, and some basil for garnish, if you like. Serve immediately with more grated cheese to pass around at the table.

Spicy and tasty!

Serves 4 to 6.

Linguini with Parmesan and Provolone Cubes

Linguini con Cubetti di Parmigiano e Provolone

1 pound linguini pasta
1/2 cup Parmesan cheese, cut into small cubes
1/2 cup provolone cheese, cut into small cubes
2 medium garlic cloves, minced
1/3 cup pignoli nuts, (pine nuts)
1 cup sun-dried tomatoes, packed in olive oil, drained and coarsely chopped

1/2 cup extra-virgin olive oil
2 tablespoons capers packed in water, rinsed, and drained
1/2 cup packed fresh basil leaves, coarsely chopped
1/3 cup grated Parmesan cheese for serving
Salt and pepper to taste and 1/2 teaspoon of freshly ground black pepper for sprinkling (optional but better)

Heat a large frying pan on medium-high heat. Add 2 tablespoons of olive oil and the garlic. Sauté the garlic lightly; lower the heat to medium and add the sun-dried tomatoes, pignoli nuts, capers, basil, salt and pepper to taste. Continue to cook the sauce about 15 minutes longer. Turn the heat off, add the Parmesan and provolone cubes, and set aside.

Cook the pasta according to package directions. When the pasta is cooked, take out 1/4 cup of the pasta water before draining it. Once drained, put the pasta back in the same pan. Add the sauce, the cubed cheeses, along with the pasta water, mix everything well, and transfer to a serving dish.

Sprinkle the top generously with some grated Parmesan cheese, the 1/2 teaspoon freshly ground black pepper if using, and a drizzle of extra virgin olive oil. Stir and serve.

Serves 4 to 6.

Bow Tie Pasta with Olive Pesto

Farfalle con Pesto d'Olive

1 pound bow tie pasta*
2 -1/2 cups kalamata olives
1/4 cup pignoli nuts
2 medium garlic cloves, minced
1/3 cup sun-dried tomatoes in olive oil,
well drained and coarsely chopped
2 tablespoons capers, rinsed and drained
3/4 cup Parmesan cheese, shredded
3/4 cup extra virgin olive oil, more for drizzling
1/2 cup parsley leaves, coarsely chopped
1 tablespoon freshly ground black pepper

*Do not add any salt to the pasta water or the sauce, as the olives are already salted.

Cook pasta according to package directions. In the meantime, in a food processor, add 2 cups of the olives, pignoli nuts, garlic, half of the parsley, sun-dried tomatoes, capers, black pepper, cheese, olive oil, and process all until smooth.

When the pasta is cooked, reserve 1 cup of the pasta water, before draining it. Put the pasta back in the same pan, add all the ingredients from the food processor and about 1/2 cup of the pasta water. Gently stir to make sure the pasta and sauce are well combined. Add a little more water if it seems too thick and stir.

Transfer it to a serving dish, and garnish with the remaining olives, a few pieces of sun-dried tomatoes the remaining parsley, a good sprinkle of freshly ground black pepper, and a good drizzle of olive oil. Serve at once. Delicious especially if you like olives!

Serves 4 to 6.

Ravioli in a Butter and Sage Sauce

Ravioli con salsa di Burro e Salvia

Dough recipe:

**2 cups flour (more flour as needed)
2 eggs
1 teaspoon salt
1 teaspoon extra-virgin olive oil
3 to 4 tablespoons of water (more if needed)**

On a wooden board, add 2 cups flour and the salt. Make a well and add the 2 eggs and the olive oil. Start beating the eggs and the olive oil with a fork and work into the flour. Add the water, one tablespoon at a time, and start kneading until you achieve a nice, smooth dough, which should take about 10 minutes or so. When done, wrap the dough in cling wrap, and set aside to rest while you prepare the filling.

Filling:

**1 pound ricotta cheese
1/2 teaspoon salt or to taste
1/4 teaspoon freshly ground black pepper or to taste
1/4 pound of either ground veal or beef (according to your taste)
1/2 cup Parmesan cheese (plus more for sprinkling)
About 20 sage leaves
1 stick of butter**

In a bowl, mix together ricotta, Parmesan cheese, the ground meat of your choice, and salt and pepper. Mix everything well, and set aside.

At this point, divide the dough in half and wrap the other half so that it won't dry out. Sprinkle some flour on a wooden board and roll the dough into a very thin rectangular sheet. Place teaspoons of filling at about 4 inches in from the edge and 2 inches apart, then fold the dough over the filling. Press down on each side of the filling with your fingers to remove any air, then cut with your favorite ravioli cutter, round or square. Press down all around the edge of each ravioli with a fork to make sure it is well sealed. Continue with the rest of the dough in the same manner.

Bring about 6 to 8 quarts of salted water to a rolling boil. Gently put the ravioli in and cook until they come up to the surface; keep cooking for about 30 seconds more. Carefully scoop them out with a large slotted spoon. Place in a colander very gently to make sure they are completely drained. Gently transfer to a serving platter and keep warm

Heat the butter in a small skillet on medium-low heat. When the butter has melted, add the sage leaves, and continue to sauté for about 1 minute longer or so, in order to flavor the butter with the sage. Drizzle that delicious sage butter sauce all over the ravioli; add the sage leaves for garnish, sprinkle some Parmesan cheese on top, and serve at once.

Note: You can also replace the butter sage sauce with tomato sauce if you prefer. Either one is equally delicious!

Enjoy!

Serves 4 to 6.

Fettuccine Alfredo Clelia Style

Fettuccine Alfredo alla Clelia

1 pound fettuccine pasta
1 stick of butter, room temperature
1 (16-ounce) container sour cream
1 cup freshly grated Parmesan cheese (preferably Reggiano)
Salt and freshly ground black pepper to taste
A few sprigs fresh parsley or chives, chopped

Cook fettuccine according to package directions. When the pasta is cooked, take out 1/4 cup of the pasta water before draining. In the same pan, turn the heat down to simmer, and add the butter and the sour cream. Mix gently until well combined. Add the fettuccine back in the pan and gently stir in some of the pasta water if needed; continue to cook until everything is heated through, then turn the heat off. Add the Parmesan cheese, adjust the seasoning if needed, gently toss everything again, and transfer to a serving bowl.

Add the chopped parsley or chives for garnish, and serve immediately with more cheese, and freshly ground black pepper to pass around at the table.

One of my father's favorite dishes!

Serves 4 to 6.

Soup Recipes

Pasta and Bean Soup

Pasta e Fagioli

1 pound dry cannellini beans (Italian beans)
1 fresh sprig rosemary,
1 fresh sprig thyme,
1 fresh bay leaf

1 tablespoon extra virgin olive oil
1 cup pasta such as small elbows, ditalini, or small shells

Check beans over and discard any little pebbles or grains. Rinse with cold water. Place the beans in a large bowl and fill with enough cold water to cover the beans by 3 to 4 inches. Let soak overnight.

The next day, drain the beans, and put them into a large pot with enough cold water to cover the beans, by about 4 to 5 inches. Tie together the rosemary, thyme, and the bay leaf with cooking string, and add to the beans along with the tablespoon of oil. Cover the pan, and turn the heat to medium-high. As soon as the pan starts to boil, lower the heat to medium-low, and cook the beans covered, for about 1 hour or until the beans are tender, stirring occasionlly. When cooked, turn the heat off, and leave the pan on the stove.

While the beans are cooking make the soffritto.

1/4 ounce of salt pork, minced
1 tablespoon extra virgin olive oil
1 small onion, chopped
1 large garlic clove, chopped
2 celery stalks, chopped
1 small carrot, chopped
1 cup of canned whole tomatoes, chopped

Heat a skillet set on medium-heat and add the oil and salt pork. Sauté until the salt pork just about melts; add the onion, garlic, celery, carrot, and continue to Sauté until the vegetables are soft and golden in color. Add the tomatoes, salt and pepper to taste, and continue to cook for about 10 to 12 more minutes, then turn off. Add the soffritto the last 15 minutes of the beans cooking time.

At this point, turn the heat back on the beans on medium-heat and remove the tied herbs. Add about 3 to 4 cups of hot water, so that you will have enough liquid to cook the pasta in with the beans. Bring the beans to a boil and add the pasta. Stir and cook the pasta according to package directions. Once the pasta is cooked, adjust the seasoning if needed, and turn the heat off. Allow the soup to rest for about 10 minutes or so. Drizzle with some extra virgin olive oil, a sprinkle of cheese and black pepper, and more cheese and pepper to pass around at the table.

Serves 6 to 8.

Lentil Soup with Sausage

Zuppa di Lenticchie

1 pound green lentils
1/3 cup barley
6 to 8 cups water
2 tablespoons extra virgin olive oil
4 to 5 Italian sweet sausages, chopped small
2 medium onions, chopped
1 large garlic clove, chopped

5 carrots, chopped
5 celery stalks, chopped
1 cup crushed tomatoes
1 teaspoon dry mustard
Romano or Parmesan grated cheese
Salt and freshly ground black pepper

Heat a soup pan on medium-high heat, and add 1 tablespoon of olive oil and the sausage. Sauté the sausage just until golden all over. When done take the sausage out and put in a dish, cover and set aside. Using the same soup pan, lower the heat to medium, add the onions, garlic, carrots, celery, mustard, and salt and pepper to taste. Cook for about 10 minutes or so stirring often. Stir in the tomatoes, turn the heat down to medium-low, and continue to cook uncovered while you rinse the lentils and barley.

Check the lentils and barley and discard any little pebbles or grains. Rinse both well in cold water and drain; add to the soup pan along with about 6 to 8 cups of water, cover and turn the heat up to medium high. As soon as the pan starts to boil, turn the heat down to medium-low. Add the sausage and continue to cook until the lentils and barley are cooked and soft. Adjust the seasoning if needed; transfer to a serving bowl or tureen, drizzle with some extra virgin olive oil, and serve with some hot crusty bread, and some grated cheese to pass around at the table.

Sooo good on a cold night!

Serves 8 to 10.

Escarole and Little Meatballs

Scarola e Polpettine

3 to 4 escarole heads, depending on size
2-1/2 to 3 quarts chicken broth
1 pound ground veal
1/3 cup seasoned breadcrumbs
1/2 cup Parmesan cheese
1 small garlic clove, minced
2 eggs
4 to 5 thyme sprigs, leaves only
Salt and freshly ground black pepper to taste
1 tablespoon extra virgin olive oil

In a large bowl, add the ground veal, breadcrumbs, cheese, garlic, thyme, salt and pepper, and eggs. Mix everything until well combined. Shape the meatballs the size of a cocktail meatball, and set aside.

Cut the top off the escarole and chop coarsely. Rinse it in cold water a few times to make sure it is free of dirt, then drain. Add the chicken broth to a soup pan, and turn the heat on to medium-high. Bring the broth to a rapid boil, add the escarole, lower the heat to medium, and cover the pan. Cook and push the escarole down with a spoon every so often, as it tends to float to the top.

Cook for about 15 minutes or so, then gently stir in the meatballs. Continue to cook with the heat still on medium for about 15 to 20 minutes longer, stirring occasionally. Adjust the seasoning if needed and turn the heat off. Transfer to a soup tureen, add a sprinkle of Parmesan cheese, and a drizzle of extra virgin olive oil. Serve nice and hot with some more Parmesan cheese to pass around at the table.

Serves 4 to 6.

Escarole and Cannellini Beans

Scarola e Fagioli Cannellini

3 cups Cannellini beans (Italian beans)
3 to 4 strips pancetta or bacon, chopped
3 to 4 escarole heads, depending on size
4 large garlic cloves, slightly crushed
1/2 teaspoon red pepper flakes (optional but better)

6 tablespoons extra virgin olive oil
1 small onion, chopped
1 rib celery, chopped
1/3 cup grated Pecorino Romano cheese
Salt and freshly ground black pepper

Check the beans to make sure there are no little pebbles or grains and rinse in cold water. Place in a large bowl with enough cold water to cover the beans by 2 to 3 inches or so, and soak them overnight.

The next day heat 1 tablespoon of olive oil in a soup pan on medium-high heat. Add the pancetta or bacon, the onion, celery, and one of the garlic cloves. Sauté for about 1 to 2 minutes; add the beans and enough water to cover the beans by about 3 inches. Bring to a boil, and then lower the heat to medium-low. Cover and cook for about 1 hour, or until the beans are soft, stirring occasionally.

While the beans are cooking, cut the top off the escarole and chop coarsely. Rinse well in cold water to make sure it is free of dirt, then drain. Add two quarts of water and some salt to a large pan. Bring to a rapid boil and add the escarole. Cook and push the escarole down with a spoon every so often as it tends to float to the top. Cook for about 15 minutes or until tender, then drain. Immediately add the escarole to the bean pan, mix all well, and turn the heat down to simmer.

In the meantime, in a small frying pan, set on medium-heat, add about 4 tablespoons of olive oil, the remaining garlic cloves, and the red pepper flakes if using. Sauté just until the garlic turns golden and fragrant, about 35 to 45 seconds, then remove.

Stir the flavored olive oil into the soup pan; turn the heat down to medium-low, and adjust the seasoning if needed. Continue to cook just until the soup comes to a slow boil, and the flavors are blended together, about 8 to 10 minutes longer, then turn the heat off. Transfer to a soup tureen, sprinkle with some cheese, some freshly ground black pepper, and a drizzle of olive oil. Serve with some hot crusty bread and more cheese to pass around at the table.

Serve 4 to 6.

Zucchini Soup

Zuppa di Zucchine

8 to 10 small zucchini
1 tablespoon extra-virgin olive oil
2 pats butter
Salt and freshly ground black pepper to taste
1 cup grated Parmesan or Romano cheese
1 cup basil leaves, coarsely chopped
1/3 cup parsley leaves, coarsely chopped
5 eggs
1 1/2 quarts chicken broth
12 to 16 ounces croutons

Scrub and rinse the zucchini to make sure that they are free of sand. Chop them into medium cubes. In a large soup pan, add the olive oil, the butter and the zucchini. Sauté for about 5 to 6 minutes on medium-high heat until lightly golden. Add the chicken broth, lower the heat to medium, and bring to a boil.

In the meantime, beat the eggs in a bowl; stir in the basil, parsley, cheese, freshly ground black pepper and mix all well. Add the egg mixture to the chicken broth, stirring continually until the eggs cook through, about 8 to 10 minutes. Taste and adjust the seasoning if needed.

Transfer the soup to a large bowl or tureen. Serve with the croutons, and more cheese and freshly ground black pepper to pass around at the table.

Serves 4 to 6.

Poultry Recipes

Important!

Never eat undercooked poultry. Poultry must be cooked all the way through. If it is even the least bit pinkish, it is not cooked. Due to different cooking conditions, (stoves and size of chicken) you may need to cook the chicken longer than stated in the recipe.

There is a lot of information on the internet about the handling and cooking of chicken. It would be a good idea to check it out.

Note: To rinse or not to rinse your poultry is entirely up to you.

Chicken Piccata

Pollo Piccata

6 chicken cutlets
1 small garlic clove, minced
2 lemons, 1 sliced, and the juice and zest of the other
1/2 cup flat parsley leaves, coarsely chopped
1/3 cup capers, rinsed in cold water and drained

4 tablespoons butter
2 tablespoons extra virgin olive oil
1/3 cup dry white wine
1/2 cup chicken broth
Flour for dusting
Salt and pepper to taste

Sprinkle the cutlets with salt and pepper on both sides, then dip into flour on both sides as well, shaking off the excess. In a nonstick large skillet, set on medium-high heat, add 2 tablespoons of butter and 1 tablespoon of olive oil. Add the cutlets two or three at a time. Do not crowd them. Sauté 2 to 3 minutes on each side. When done, place them in a dish, cover and keep warm.

In the same skillet, turn the heat down to medium-low, add the rest of the butter and the olive oil. Add the garlic and sauté for about 25 to 30 seconds, then add the lemon juice, some lemon zest, parsley, capers, white wine and salt and pepper to taste. Cook for about 5 to 6 minutes until the win has evaporated, scraping up any brown bits collected in the skillet with a wooden spoon. Add the chicken broth and continue to cook until the sauce slightly thickens. Put the cutlets back in the pan, and cook just until heated through.

Arrange the cutlets on a serving platter, and pour the sauce over the top. Garnish with the lemon slices, more chopped parsley, and the rest of the lemon zest.

Serve at once.

Serves 4 to 6.

Chicken Parmesan Clelia Style

Pollo alla Parmigiana a modo mio

Start by making the sauce first:

2 large garlic cloves, crushed
2 tablespoons extra-virgin olive oil
1 (28-ounce) can of chunky or crushed tomatoes (good Italian brand)
Salt and freshly ground black pepper
1/4 teaspoon red pepper flakes (optional but better)

In a medium saucepan on medium-high heat, sauté the garlic in 2 tablespoons of olive oil just until lightly golden in color. Add the red pepper flakes if using, the tomatoes, and salt and pepper to taste. Lower the heat to medium, when the sauce starts to slightly bubble, turn the heat down to medium-low and cook uncovered for about 25 to 30 minutes, stirring occasionally. When done, cover the pan and keep aside.

6 chicken cutlets
1 cup Italian flavored breadcrumbs
2 large eggs
6 tablespoons extra virgin olive oil
1 tablespoon dry oregano
1/2 cup flat parsley leaves, coarsely chopped
1/3 cup basil leaves, coarsely chopped
1 small garlic clove, minced
3/4 cup grated Parmesan cheese
2 large balls fresh mozzarella cheese, thinly sliced
Salt and freshly ground black pepper to taste

Preheat the oven to 350 degrees.

Put the cutlets between two pieces of plastic wrap and pound to even out the thickness. Beat the eggs in a bowl, and add some salt and pepper to taste.

Pour the breadcrumbs in a flat dish and keep it next to the bowl with the eggs. Now you are ready to proceed.

Heat 4 tablespoons of olive oil in a nonstick large skillet on medium-high heat. Dip the cutlets one at a time, first in the eggs, then in the breadcrumbs. When the olive oil is hot, place 3 cutlets at a time in the hot skillet. Do not crowd them or they will not brown properly. Cook about 2 to 3 minutes per side, depending on the thickness of the cutlets. Add more olive oil as needed. Place them in a dish lined with paper towels as they get done.

Spread some sauce in a large roasting pan, enough to cover the bottom of the pan. Place the cutlets on top of the sauce in a single layer. Sprinkle them with some garlic, oregano, parsley, basil, a generous sprinkle of Parmesan cheese, the mozzarella slices, more sauce, and the rest of the Parmesan cheese over all.

Cover the roasting pan with some foil, and place in the heated oven. Cook for about 12 to 15 minutes or until the mozzarella starts to melt, and the cutlets are heated through.

Remove from the oven, transfer to a serving platter, and serve at once.

Serves 6.

Chicken Cutlets with Marsala

Cotolette di Pollo con Marsala

6 chicken cutlets
1 tablespoon extra virgin olive oil
4 to 5 tablespoons butter (more if needed)
1/4 cup flour
1 cup sweet Marsala wine
2 tablespoon Worcestershire sauce

3 large Portobello mushrooms, sliced
1 clove garlic, minced
Salt and freshly ground black pepper to taste
2 to 3 sprigs fresh thyme leaves lightly chopped
2 to 3 sprigs fresh Italian parsley leaves chopped

Heat the olive oil and 2 tablespoons of butter in a large skillet on medium-high heat. Season the cutlets with salt and pepper on both sides and dip in flour on both sides as well, shaking off the excess. Place the cutlets in the skillet a few at a time. Do not crowd them. Sauté for about 2 to 3 minutes on each side or until golden and cooked through. When done, put in a dish, cover and keep warm.

Add the rest of the butter to the same skillet. Lower the heat to medium, add the mushrooms and cook for about 6 to 7 minutes or so stirring often. Add the garlic, thyme, parsley, and stir quickly so that the garlic does not burn. Add the Marsala wine, and the Worcestershire sauce. Turn the heat back up to medium-high, and continue to cook and stir for about 5 more minutes until the alcohol evaporates and the sauce slightly thickens.

Put the chicken back in the pan and continue to cook for a few more minutes just until the chicken is heated through. Transfer the chicken to a serving platter, pour all that delicious sauce on top, garnish with more parsley and thyme leaves, and serve at once.

Serves 4 to 6.

Chicken Cutlets with Prosciutto

Cotolette di Pollo con Prosciutto

6 chicken cutlets
1 tablespoon olive oil
3 tablespoons butter
1/4 cup flour
1/4 pound prosciutto, sliced
1 large mozzarella ball, thinly sliced

1/3 cup heavy cream
1/2 cup sweet Marsala wine
6 sprigs of fresh thyme, leaves only
Salt and freshly ground black pepper to taste

Season the chicken with salt and pepper, dip lightly in the flour and shake off excess. Heat the olive oil and butter in a large skillet on medium-high heat. Cook the chicken until golden and cooked through; about 2 to 3 minutes per side, depending on the thickness of the cutlets. When done, transfer to a dish, and sprinkle each cutlet generously with the thyme leaves, a slice of mozzarella, a slice of prosciutto and set aside.

Add the Marsala wine to the same skillet and cook over medium-high heat, scraping up any brown bits collected in the frying pan with a wooden spoon. Cook the sauce for 1 to 2 minutes. Add the cream; reduce the heat to medium, and continue cooking until slightly thickened.

Add the cutlets back in the pan in a single layer. Turn the heat down to medium-low; cover the pan, and cook just long enough to heat the chicken through and melt the mozzarella slightly, about 2 minutes longer or so. Arrange the chicken in a serving platter; pour that delicious sauce over it, and serve.

If you like to serve it on a bed of spinach as in the picture, check out the recipe below:

Sautéd Spinach:

3 pats of butter
1 garlic clove, minced
2 pounds baby spinach, rinsed and spun dry
Salt to taste

Heat a medium skillet on medium-heat and melt the butter. Add the minced garlic and sauté for about 15 seconds or so stirring to make sure the garlic does not burn. Add the spinach, a sprinkle of salt, stir, and cover. Cook just long enough for the spinach to wilt, about 1 to 2 minutes. Arrange in a serving platter as a bed and place the chicken over it.

Serves 4 to 6.

Chicken Thighs with Mushrooms and Cognac

Cosce di Pollo con Funghi e Cognac

12 chicken thighs (bone in)
20 garlic cloves, crushed
1 large shallot, minced
3 Portobello mushrooms, sliced
3 tablespoons extra virgin olive oil

3 pats of butter
1/2 cup flour
1/2 cup brandy or cognac
1/2 cup heavy cream
Salt and freshly ground black pepper to taste

Heat a large skillet on medium-high heat and add 2 tablespoons of olive oil and 2 pats of butter. Sprinkle the thighs with salt and pepper on both sides, dip lightly in the flour, shaking off the excess. Add the thighs to the skillet a few at a time. Brown all over, for about 5 to 6 minutes per side, depending on the size of the thighs, or until cooked through. Take them out and put in a dish lined with paper towels, as they get done, and set aside.

When all done, add 1 more tablespoon of olive oil and 1 pat of butter to the same skillet. Turn the heat to medium-high, add all the garlic cloves and sauté, stirring often, until the garlic turns to a light golden color; add the shallot and continue to Sauté until the shallot become slightly soft. Add the mushrooms, stir and continue to cook for about 8 to 10 minutes longer, stirring often. Add the brandy, and continue to cook until the alcohol evaporates, about 2 more minutes.

Stir in the cream and simmer for 5 to 6 minutes longer until the sauce slightly thickens. Add the thighs back in the skillet and cook for about 2 to 3 minutes longer; just until the thighs are heated through. Adjust the seasoning if needed, and transfer to a serving dish; pour that delicious sauce over it, and serve at once.

Serves 6 to 8.

Chicken Cutlets with Dried Apricots and Vermouth

Cotolette di Pollo con Albicocche Secche e Vermut

6 chicken cutlets
2 tablespoons extra-virgin olive oil
4 pats of butter
Salt and freshly ground black pepper
1/2 cup flour for dipping
2 large garlic cloves, chopped
2 tablespoons Worcestershire sauce

4 to 5 sprigs fresh thyme, leaves only
3 large Portobello mushrooms, sliced
1/3 cup dried apricots (organic preferred)
1/2 cup sweet red vermouth

Heat 2 tablespoons of olive oil and 2 pats of butter in a large skillet over medium-high heat. Salt and pepper the cutlets on both sides, and dip each one in flour, shaking off the excess. Add the cutlets to the skillet a few at a time. Do not crowd them. Cook on each side for about 2 to 3 minutes. When the chicken is cooked, take it out of the skillet; cover and set aside.

In the same skillet, still on medium-high heat, add the garlic and sauté for about 35 seconds. Add the mushrooms and thyme, and sauté for about 2 minutes, and then add the apricots. Continue to sauté for about 1 to 2 minutes longer; put in the vermouth, Worcestershire sauce, and 2 pats of butter. Continue to cook the sauce until slightly thickened. Add the chicken back in the pan, adjust the seasoning if needed, and cook for 1 to 2 minutes longer or just until the chicken is heated through.

Transfer the chicken to a serving dish, and pour all that delicious sauce over it. Sprinkle some more thyme leaves for garnish and serve.

Serves 4 to 6.

Chicken with Gorgonzola Sauce

Pollo con Gorgonzola

6 whole bonless chicken breasts split in half
2 tablespoons extra-virgin olive oil
3 pats butter
6 to 8 ounces gorgonzola cheese
1/2 cup heavy cream
1/4 cup cognac or brandy
Salt and pepper to taste
Flour for dusting
2 or 3 sprigs Italian parsley leaves, chopped
3 sprigs thyme leaves, chopped

Heat a large skillet on medium-high heat and add the olive oil and 2 pats of butter. Sprinkle the cutlets with salt and pepper and dip them in flour, shaking off the excess. Add to the skillet and start browning the cutlets a few at a time. Do not overcrowd them. Cook for about 2 to 3 minutes per side or until the chicken is golden and cooked through. When done, transfer to a dish, cover, and keep warm.

Discard any leftover fat in the pan. Keep the heat on medium-high and add the cognac. Scrape any bits left in the pan with a wooden spoon. Lower the heat to medium and add the rest of the butter. Continue to stir until the butter melts. Add the gorgonzola cheese and the cream and continue to stir until the cheese has melted and the sauce has thickened to a nice smooth consistency. Taste and adjust the seasoning if needed.

Add the chicken back in the skillet. Lower the heat to medium-low and continue to cook for 1 to 2 minutes longer or until the chicken is heated through. Transfer the chicken to a serving platter, and pour that luscious sauce over it. Sprinkle some chopped parsley or thyme for garnish and serve immediately.

You can also serve this chicken with some baby carrots as shown in the picture. Bring a quart of salted water to a boil. Add the carrots and cook for about 6 to 8 minutes. Drain, sprinkle some freshly ground black pepper, about 3 tablespoons extra-virgin olive oil, and a sprinkle of chopped parsley. Stir and serve.

Serves 6 to 8.

Chicken Cutlets with Pizza Sauce

Cotolette di Pollo alla Pizzaiola

6 chicken cutlets
2 pounds cherry tomatoes, cut in half
5 to 6 tablespoons extra-virgin olive oil
4 garlic cloves, 1 minced and 3 crushed
1 tablespoon dried oregano
1/2 cup Italian parsley leaves, roughly chopped
8 to 10 basil leaves, torn
1/2 cup Pecorino Romano cheese
1/2 teaspoon red pepper flakes (optional but better)
Salt and freshly ground black pepper to taste

Heat 2 tablespoons of extra-virgin olive oil in a large skillet on medium-high heat. Add the 3 large crushed garlic cloves and sauté, stirring until lightly golden all over. Add the tomatoes and lower the heat to medium-low. Sprinkle some salt, freshly ground black pepper to taste, the red pepper flakes if using, and some basil leaves. Continue to cook uncovered, stirring occasionally while you cook the chicken.

Heat 3 tablespoons of olive oil in a large frying pan. Sprinkle the chicken with some salt and pepper on both sides, Cook 2 to 3 cutlets at a time for about 2 to 3 minutes per side, or until golden and cooked through. When done, transfer to a dish, cover, and keep warm. Drain any excess olive oil left in the frying pan and wipe the pan clean with paper towels.

In the same frying pan, spread some of the tomato sauce on the bottom of the pan. Add the cutlets in a single layer. Sprinkle with the minced garlic, oregano, parsley, basil, freshly ground black pepper, some grated cheese, all the remaining tomato sauce, and top with the rest of the grated cheese.

Cover and cook for about 2 more minutes or so on medium-low heat in order to flavor the chicken with the sauce and spices. Transfer the chicken to a serving platter. Pour the the sauce over it and serve immediately.

Very delicious and very Neapolitan!

Serves 4 to 6.

Chicken with Ginger

Pollo con Zenzero

6 chicken cutlets
1 tablespoon freshly grated ginger
1/3 cup flour
2 to 3 tablespoons extra-virgin olive oil
2 tablespoons butter
1 medium garlic clove, minced
2 tablespoons pink and green peppercorns

2 pounds cherry tomatoes, cut in half
2 cups basil leaves
1/2 cup dry white wine
Salt and pepper to taste
1 head Boston lettuce

Heat a frying pan on medium-high heat and add the olive oil. Sprinkle the cutlets on both sides with salt and pepper; dip them in flour, and shake off the excess. Sauté in the frying pan a few at a time. Do not crowd them. Cook for about 2 to 3 minutes on each side until golden and cooked through. When done, take them out, cover and keep warm.

Wipe the same pan clean with paper towels. Turn the heat down to medium, and add the butter and minced garlic. Sauté the garlic lightly, about 30 seconds; add the pink and green peppercorns and the wine. Continue to sauté for about 1 to 2 more minutes and then add the tomatoes and basil. Turn the heat down to medium-low, and continue to cook uncovered for about 15 to 20 minutes stirring a few times.

At this point, add the chicken back in the pan and sprinkle it with the grated ginger. Cook for about 2 more minutes or so until the chicken is heated through. Place the lettuce in a serving platter to form a bed and put the chicken cutlets on top. Pour the sauce over the chicken, and serve at once.

Serves 4 to 6.

Chicken Cacciatore

Pollo alla Cacciatore

1 large chicken (5 to 6 pounds cut up)
1/2 cup flour
4 to 5 tablespoons extra-virgin olive oil
1 large onion, chopped
3 garlic cloves, chopped
3 large peppers, red, green, and yellow, seeded and sliced
1 pound white mushrooms, sliced
1 (28-ounce) can chunky or crushed tomatoes
1 cup good dry red wine
Salt and freshly ground black pepper to taste

In a large and deep frying pan, heat 2 tablespoons of the olive oil on medium-high heat. Sprinkle the chicken with some salt and pepper and dip each piece in the flour, shaking off the excess. Place the chicken in the frying pan skin side down and start browning a few pieces at a time; until golden on all sides. Do not crowd. When all done, take the chicken out of the pan, and set aside.

Wipe clean the same frying pan with paper towels. Turn the heat on medium-high; add the olive oil and the chopped onion and garlic. Stir and sauté for about 5 to 6 minutes or so. Add the peppers and mushrooms; continue to cook and stir still on medium-high heat for about 6 to 8 minutes. Stir in the tomatoes and the wine, adjust the seasoning, and continue to cook for about 15 to 20 minutes longer, uncovered.

Add the chicken back in the same frying pan, and cook covered for about 15 more minutes or until the chicken is cooked through. When done, transfer the chicken to a large serving bowl, and pour all that nice sauce and vegetables on top. Serve immediately with some delicious hot bread!

Serves 6 to 8.

Chicken Legs with Porcini and Marsala

Cosce di Pollo con Porcini e Marsala

12 chicken drumsticks
1/2 cup flour for dusting
4 tablespoons extra-virgin olive oil
1 (12-ounce) package dry porcini mushrooms
6 large garlic cloves, crushed
1 cup sweet Marsala wine (good Italian brand)
2 tablespoons Worcestershire sauce
3 pats of butter
1/2 cup flat parsley leaves, coarsely chopped
Salt and freshly ground black pepper to taste

Brush the sand off the porcini mushrooms and put them in a bowl. Cover with warm water and set aside. Sprinkle the drumsticks with salt and pepper. Dip each one in flour and shake off the excess. In a large skillet, heat the olive oil to medium-high heat. Add the drumsticks a few at a time, and lower the heat to medium. Cook until golden brown all over and cooked through; about 7 to 8 minutes. Take them out of the pan as they get done. When all done, cover and set aside.

Drain all the fat collected in the skillet and add 2 pats of butter. When the butter has melted, add the garlic and sauté on medium heat until the garlic is lightly golden. Squeeze the water out of the mushrooms, making sure they are free of sand and add to the skillet. Continue to sauté the garlic and the mushrooms for about 5 minutes or so. Sprinkle some salt and pepper to taste; add the Marsala, the Worcestershire sauce, the remaining pat of butter, salt, and freshly ground black pepper. Cook the sauce for about 10 minutes uncovered, until the sauce starts to reduce and slightly thickens.

Add the chicken back in the skillet, and continue to cook covered on medium-low heat; until the chicken is heated through, about 10 minutes longer or so. Adjust the seasoning if needed, sprinkle with the parsley, and serve at once.

Serves 4 to 6.

Stuffed Chicken Thighs

Cosce di Pollo Ripiene

12 boneless and skinless chicken thighs
1-1/2 cups Italian seasoned breadcrumbs
3 eggs, beaten
1/2 cup Romano cheese
1 small garlic clove, minced
2 tablespoons fresh thyme leaves, minced
1/4 cup fresh flat parsley leaves, chopped
1/4 cup fresh oregano leaves, chopped
1/4 cup water
4 to 5 tablespoons extra-virgin olive oil
4 ounces sun-dried tomatoes in olive oil, drained and cut julienned
Salt and freshly ground black pepper to taste
Cooking twine

Preheat oven to 375 degrees.

Put the chicken thighs flat on a board and sprinkle a little salt and pepper on top.
In a medium bowl, add 1/2 cup of the breadcrumbs, the cheese, garlic, thyme, parsley, oregano, sun-dried tomatoes, water, the olive oil, and mix everything well. Place 1 to 2 tablespoons of the stuffing on top of each thigh. Roll each thigh tightly and secure with cooking twine.

Put the remaining cup of the breadcrumbs into a flat dish, and the beaten eggs into a bowl. Dip each chicken roll first in the eggs, then in the breadcrumbs. Brush a 9 × 11 roasting pan with some olive oil. Put all the rolls in the roasting pan in a single layer; sprinkle the top generously with some olive oil, and place in the oven. Cook for about 20 to 25 minutes until golden in color and cooked all the way through. Let the thighs rest for about 5 minutes, remove the cooking twine, and serve with your favorite side dishes.

Serves 6 to 8.

Chicken Cutlets with White Wine

Cotolette di Pollo al Vino Bianco

4 chicken cutlets
3 tablespoons of extra virgin olive oil
4 tablespoons butter
1/3 cup flour
1 large garlic clove, thinly sliced
1/2 cup dry white wine
1 sprig Italian flat parsley leaves, chopped
1 small lemon, zest and juice
1 pound, baby arugula
Salt and freshly ground black pepper to taste

Sprinkle the cutlets with some salt and pepper on both sides; dip in the flour and set aside. Heat a nonstick large skillet on medium-high heat and add 1 tablespoon of olive oil and 2 tablespoons of butter. When the olive oil is hot and the butter has melted, add the cutlets to the skillet. Sauté for about 2 to 3 minutes per side until cooked through. When done, put them in a plate, cover and keep warm.

In the same skillet, lower the heat to medium and add the other 2 tablespoons of butter and the sliced garlic. Sauté to a light golden color for about 20 to 25 seconds or so. Add the wine, salt and pepper to taste, and continue to cook for a few more minutes until the alcohol evaporates, and the sauce slightly thickens. Put the cutlets back in the skillet for about 1 to 2 minutes longer or so, just enough to heat through. Turn the heat off, cover, and keep warm.

Rinse and spin dry the arugula; place in a bowl, and add the lemon juice, 2 tablespoons of olive oil, salt and pepper to taste and mix well. Arrange the arugula as a bed on a serving platter and place the chicken cutlets on top. Pour all the sauce on top, and sprinkle with the lemon zest and some parsley, before serving.

Serves 4.

Chicken Breasts with Tuna Sauce

Petti di Pollo con Salsa di Tonno

4 boneless and skinless chicken breasts,
3 tablespoons extra-virgin olive oil
3 pats of butter
1 medium onion, chopped
1 stalk celery, chopped
1 medium carrot, chopped
1 small garlic clove, minced
2 tablespoons capers, rinsed in cold water and drained
1 tablespoon lemon juice
1 whole lemon sliced for garnish
1 cup dry white wine

1 sprig fresh rosemary, needles only, finely minced
1 sprig sage, leaves only, finely chopped
1 (6-ounce) can of tuna packed in olive oil, drained (good Italian brand)
1/2 cup mayonnaise
Salt and freshly ground black pepper to taste
1/2 cup flour for dusting the chicken
One bunch large arugula leaves, rinsed and spun-dried

Preheat the oven to 400 degrees.

Heat an ovenproof skillet on medium-high heat and add 1 tablespoon of olive oil and 1 pat of butter. Sprinkle the chicken breasts with salt and freshly ground black pepper on both sides. Dip in the flour; shake off the excess, and add to the skillet a few at a time. Cook each side for about 2 to 3 minutes. Place them in a dish as they get done, cover, and set aside.

Wipe the same skillet clean with some paper towels. Add 1 pat of butter, 1 tablespoon of olive oil, the onion, garlic, capers, vegetables and herbs; sauté until the onion and vegetables are soft 6 to 8 minutes. Stir in the tuna and lemon juice, and cook and stir 1 to 2 minutes longer until all the flavors combine. Add the wine, stir, and continue to cook about 5 to 6 more minutes until the sauce slightly thickens, and the alcohol evaporates.

Add the chicken back to the skillet, and spoon some of the sauce over it. Place the skillet in the heated oven for about 8 to 10 minutes or so, until the chicken is flavored with the sauce and cooked through.

When done, take the skillet out of the oven. Remove the chicken out of the skillet to a dish, cover and set aside. Leave the sauce to cool in the skillet **completely.** Once cooled, put all the sauce in a food processor and process until creamy. When done, pour it into a bowl, and stir in the mayonnaise, just until everything is well blended together.

Place the chicken breasts on a board and slice them diagonally. Spread the arugula in a serving platter in order to form a bed. Place the chicken slices overlapping on top of the arugula and spoon some of that delicious sauce over the chicken. Garnish with some lemon slices and serve the rest of the sauce on the side.

This recipe can be served at room temperature or even cold.

Enjoy!

Serves 4 to 6.

Chicken Thighs alla Clelia

Cosce di Pollo a Modo Mio

12 chicken thighs, bone in
2 to 3 eggs, beaten
1 cup seasoned breadcrumbs (more if needed)
1/3 cup Bayou Cajun Seasoning
1/2 cup extra-virgin olive oil
Salt and freshly ground black pepper to taste

Preheat oven to 350 degrees.

Beat the eggs in a bowl, and sprinkle with a little salt and pepper. Put the breadcrumbs in a flat dish and place beside the bowl with the eggs. Dip each thigh first in the eggs and then in the breadcrumbs. Continue until all done.

Brush the bottom and sides of a 9 x 13 roasting pan with the olive oil; add the thighs in a single layer. Sprinkle the thighs generously with some Cajun seasoning and a good drizzle of olive oil. Put the pan in the preheated oven, uncovered, and cook for about 45 minutes to 1 hour, depending on the size of the thighs. Cook until golden brown and cooked all the way through.

Serve immediately nice and hot with your favorite side dishes!

Serves 8 to 10.

Stuffed Turkey Breast

Petto di Tacchino Imbottito

4 to 5 pounds boneless turkey breast
3 sweet Italian sausages, casings removed
1/4 pound ground beef
3 tablespoons extra virgin olive oil
1 medium onion, chopped
1 large garlic clove, minced
2 eggs
1 tablespoon Grey Poupon mustard
1/2 cup mixed fresh herb leaves, finely chopped (such as parsley, thyme, marjoram, and oregano)
1/2 cup Italian seasoned breadcrumbs
1/2 cup heavy cream
Salt and freshly ground black pepper to taste
Cooking twine for tying

Preheat oven to 350 degrees.

Heat 1 tablespoon of olive oil in a skillet on medium-high heat and sauté the onion. When the onion is translucent, add the garlic, stir, and continue to sauté for about 35 seconds more. Add the sausage and beef and continue to cook and stir just for 2 to 3 minutes until the meat is mixed well with the onion and garlic and no longer pink.

Put everything in a large bowl. Add the mustard, herbs, eggs, breadcrumbs, cream, and salt and freshly ground black pepper to taste. Mix everything well.

Place the turkey roast on a board, and open it flat like a book or have the butcher do it for you.. Place between two pieces of clear wrap and pound with a mallet to make sure the meat is of an even thickness. Sprinkle it with some salt and freshly ground black pepper to taste.

Spread all the stuffing evenly on top of the turkey breast and then start rolling the breast like a jellyroll very tight. Tie the roll with cooking twine about 2 inches apart until the roast is well secured and the stuffing is all inside.

Place the roast in a roasting pan, brush all over with some olive oil and put it in the oven. Cook for about 1 and 1/2 hours or so, or until the thermometer reaches 165 to 170 degrees and the roast is a nice golden color and cooked through.

Place the roast on a carving board, cover it with foil, and let it rest for about 15 minutes or so. Remove all the cooking twine before slicing. Arrange the slices on a serving platter and serve with your favorite side dishes.

Delicious and a very nice presentation especially on Thanksgiving or anytime. Also a nice alternative if you prefer white meat, and don't want to cook a whole bird!

Serves 6 to 8.

Beef, Veal, and Pork Recipes

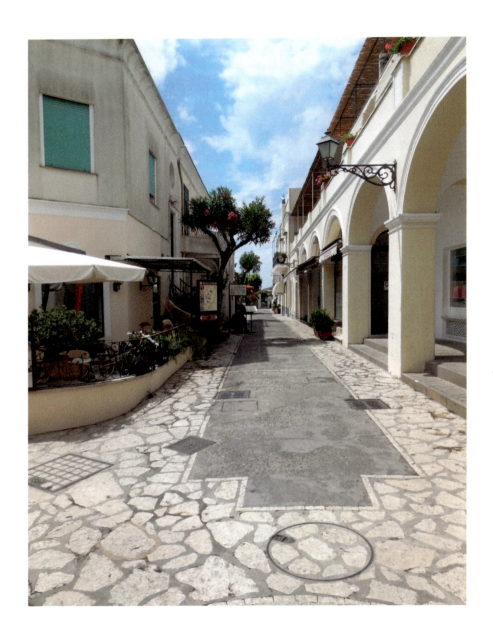

Steak Pizzaiola

Bistecca alla Pizzaiola

2 pounds cherry tomatoes cut in half
4 tablespoons extra virgin olive oil
2 pounds eye round roast thinly sliced, about 1/4 inch
4 large garlic cloves, 3 crushed and 1 minced
1/2 cup fresh basil leaves, torn
7 to 8 sprigs Italian parsley leaves, chopped
1 tablespoon dry oregano
5 to 6 sprigs fresh oregano, leaves, minced
1/2 cup grated Pecorino Romano cheese
1/4 teaspoon red pepper flakes (optional but better)
Salt and freshly ground black pepper to taste

Heat a saucepan on medium-high heat and add 2 tablespoons of olive oil and 3 crushed garlic cloves. Sauté for 30 to 35 seconds. Add the tomatoes, basil, salt, pepper, red pepper flakes if using, and stir. Lower the heat to medium-low; cook uncovered for 25 to 30 minutes, stirring occasionally while you prepare the meat.

Heat the remaining 2 tablespoons of olive oil in a large skillet on medium-high heat. When the olive oil is hot, add the meat a few slices at a time. Do not crowd the meat, or it will not brown to a nice golden color. Cook on medium-high heat for about 1 minute per side. When done place in a dish, cover, and keep warm.

Discard any olive oil left in the frying pan. Wipe the pan clean with some paper towels, and add some sauce to the pan, enough to cover the bottom of the pan. Top with a layer of the meat slices, a sprinkle of the minced garlic, a sprinkle each of parsley leaves, dry oregano, fresh oregano leaves, half of the grated cheese, and more sauce on top. Repeat the next layer in the same manner with the rest of the garlic, the herbs, the sauce and the rest of the cheese.

Cover the pan, and simmer for about 5 to 6 minutes longer, to absorb all the flavors together. Arrange the slices on a serving platter, and garnish with some more herbs.

Serve with a nice salad and some hot crusty bread!

Serves 4 to 6

Beef Rollups

Involtini di Manzo

Start by making the tomato sauce first:

2 (28-ounce) cans crushed tomatoes, good Italian brand
2 tablespoons extra virgin olive oil
4 to 5 garlic cloves, crushed
1/4 teaspoon red pepper flakes
1/2 cup basil leaves
Salt and freshly ground black pepper

Heat the olive oil in a medium size saucepan on medium-high heat. Add the garlic cloves and Sauté for about 30 to 35 seconds or until light golden in color. Add the tomatoes, red pepper flakes, salt and pepper to taste. Continue to cook uncovered for about 45 minutes or so, stirring occasionally. Add the basil leaves the last 5 minutes of the cooking time. Leave the pan on the stove covered, with the heat down to simmer, while you prepare the rollups.

4 top of the round cutlets, cut in half
1 medium size garlic clove, minced
3 tablespoons golden raisins, soaked in warm water to soften, and then drained
3 tablespoons pignoli (pine nuts)
1 -1/2 cups Italian flat leaf parsely, chopped
1 cup grated Pecorino Romano cheese
Salt and freshly ground black pepper
5 tablespoons extra virgin olive oil
Cooking twine

Ask your butcher to cut 4 top of the round cutlets, nice and thin. They should be long enough to cut in half. Once cut in half, line up the slices on a wooden board. In a bowl, mix together the minced garlic, raisins, pignoli, Romano cheese, salt, a generous amount of ground black pepper, all the parsley, and a drizzle of about 3 tablespoons of olive oil. Mix it all well, and salt and pepper the meat. Place a generous tablespoon of the mixture on each slice of the meat. Roll the meat slices jelly roll style tightly and secure with the twine or toothpicks.

Heat a skillet on medium-high heat and add about 2 tablespoons of olive oil. When the oil is hot, place just a few meat rollups at a time and Sauté all over lightly to a light golden color. Remove and place in a dish lined with paper towels, as they get done. When all done, add them to the tomato sauce. Turn the heat up to medium on the sauce pan, and continue to cook the rollups in the sauce, for about 20 minutes longer or so, stirring occasionally.

When done, cool slightly, remove the twine from the rollups, and serve as a main course or over pasta as shown in the picture.

Buon Appetito!

Yields 8

Clelia's Meatballs

Polpette alla Clelia

Start by making the sauce first:

3 (28-ounce) cans crushed tomatoes (good Italian brand)
1 tablespoon tomato paste
2 tablespoons extra-virgin olive oil
5 to 6 large garlic cloves, crushed

1/2 cup fresh basil leaves
1/4 teaspoon red pepper flakes (optional)
Salt and freshly ground black pepper to taste

Heat 2 tablespoons of olive oil in a large saucepan on medium-high heat. Add the garlic and sauté for about 30 to 35 seconds or until the garlic is a light golden color. Add the red pepper flakes if using, the tomatoes, tomato paste, and salt and pepper to taste. Lower the heat to medium-low and cook uncovered for about 1 hour or so, stirring occasionally. Stir in the basil the last 5 minutes of cooking time. Leave the pan on the stove on simmer and covered while you make the meatballs.

Meatball recipe:

2 tablespoons extra-virgin olive oil
2 pounds ground beef
1/2 pound ground pork
1/2 pound ground veal
3/4 cup Italian seasoned breadcrumbs
1 large garlic clove, finely minced
3/4 cup freshly grated Pecorino Romano cheese,
3 eggs, lightly beaten
1 cup Italian parsley leaves, chopped
1/2 cup basil leaves, chopped
1/3 cup cold water
Salt and freshly ground black pepper to taste

In a large bowl, mix all the ingredients together except the olive oil. Mix all well with your hands. Take about 3 to 4 tablespoons of the meat mixture and start shaping the meatballs. Heat the olive oil in a large non-stick skillet on medium-heat and add the meatballs in batches. Brown the meatballs on all sides to a light golden color.

As the meatballs brown, put them in a dish lined with paper towels in order to absorb any fat. When all the meatballs are done, turn the heat up to medium on the tomato saucepan and add in the meatballs. Continue to cook the meatballs in the sauce for about 25 to 30 minutes or so, gently stirring a few times, until the meatballs are cooked through. When done, serve over your favorite pasta with more sauce and cheese to pass around at the table, or as a main course.

Note: You can also use all ground beef if you prefer, and proceed with all the other ingredients in the same manner.

Makes 2 dozen or more meatballs depending on the size.

Veal Chops with Cognac and Peppercorns

Costate di Vitello con Cognac e Pepe in Grani

2 veal rib chops
2 tablespoons Dijon mustard
1/4 cup all purpose flour
1 tablespoon extra virgin olive oil
2 tablespoons butter

1/3 cup cognac
1/3 cup heavy cream
2 tablespoons mixed pepper corns
Salt to taste

Preheat the oven to 375 degrees.

Place the chops on a board and wipe any moisture off with paper towels. Spread both sides of each chop with about 1 tablespoon of mustard, and then carefully dip each one on both sides into the flour, shaking off the excess. Heat the olive oil and butter in an oven proof skillet on medium-high heat. Carefully add the chops and cook about 2 minutes per side depending on the thickness of the chops. Turn once, then place the same skillet in the preheated oven and continue to cook the chops for about 10 to 12 more minutes.

When done, carefully take the hot skillet out of the oven; remove the chops to a dish; cover and keep warm. Place the skillet back on the burner on medium-high heat and add the cognac, stirring and scraping in order to get all those nice bits collected at the bottom of the skillet. Continue to cook for about 1 to 2 minutes or so; then add the peppercorns, stir in the cream, and continue to cook until the cream lightly thickens. Taste, and season with salt if needed.

Add the chops back in the skillet, and cook just until heated through. Transfer to a serving dish; pour all that delicious sauce over the top, and serve at once with your favorite side dishes.

Serves 2.

Veal Cutlets alla Clelia

Cotolette di Vitello a Modo Mio

6 medium veal cutlets
1/2 cup extra-virgin olive oil (more as needed)
1 cup seasoned breadcrumbs
2 to 3 eggs, well beaten
3 to 4 large fresh tomatoes, sliced about 1/4 inch
2 large fresh mozzarella balls, sliced about 1/4 inch
12 to 14 slices of prosciutto, preferably imported
20 fresh basil leaves, chopped
2 to 3 sprigs fresh thyme, leaves only, minced
2 to 3 sprigs oregano, leaves only, chopped
Salt and freshly ground black pepper to taste

In a small bowl, add 1/3 cup of the olive oil, basil, thyme, oregano, and salt and pepper to taste. Mix well and set the marinade aside to top the meat before serving.

Heat the remaining olive oil in a large skillet on medium-high heat. Pound the veal cutlets between two pieces of wax paper to make sure the meat is of an even thickness. Sprinkle the cutlets on both sides with salt and pepper. Dip each cutlet first in the eggs then in the breadcrumbs. Sauté a few at a time. Do not crowd the cutlets. Cook for about 1 to 2 minutes on each side. As they get done, place in a dish lined with paper towels to absorb any fat. When all cooked, discard any olive oil left in the pan and wipe the pan clean with some paper towels.

Bring that same skillet to the working counter along with the other ingredients in order to start assembling the cutlets. Wrap one or two slices of prosciutto around each slice of mozzarella in order to completely cover it. Place the covered mozzarella on top of each cutlet, and place a slice of tomato on top of the mozzarella.

When they are all completed, put the stacks of cutlets back in the same skillet. Put the skillet back on the stove on medium-low with a cover. Heat the cutlets until the mozzarella starts to slightly melt and the tomatoes and cutlets are heated through, about 6 to 8 minutes.

Transfer the cutlets to a serving platter, and top each cutlet with a teaspoon of the prepared marinade, as shown in the picture. Serve immediately with your favorite side dish.

Delicious and a great presentation!

Serves 6.

Stuffed Veal Chops

Costate di Vitello Ripiene

2 veal rib chops
1/2 cup minced fresh herbs, leaves only, such as thyme, marjoram, basil, parsley, etc.
1 small garlic clove, minced
2 tablespoons pignoli (pine nuts)
1/4 cup grated Pecorino Romano cheese
2 tablespoons extra virgin olive oil for the stuffing
2 ounces Gorgonzola cheese, sliced or
2 ounces Fontina cheese, sliced
2 tablespoons butter

2 tablespoons extra virgin olive oil for frying
1/4 cup flour
Salt and freshly ground black pepper to taste

Sauce ingredients:

2 pats butter
1/4 cup dry white wine
1/3 cup chicken broth
Some chopped herbs, leaves only, such as thyme, marjoram, parsley, basil
1 teaspoon flour
Salt and freshly ground black pepper to taste

Heat the oven to 400 degrees.

In a small bowl, mix together the herbs, garlic, Romano cheese, pignoli nuts, the olive oil, and salt and pepper to taste.

Wipe any moisture off the chops with paper towels. Cut each chop along the side to form a pocket. Insert about 1 to 2 tablespoons of the herb mixture into each pocket, and 2 to 3 small slices of gorgonzola cheese or Fontina cheese into each pocket as well. Close the pockets with toothpicks, making sure the stuffing stays in and the pockets are sealed. Sprinkle the chops with salt and pepper to taste and then dip each chop lightly in the flour, shaking off the excess.

Heat an oven proof large skillet to medium-high heat and add the butter and olive oil. When the butter has melted, add the chops. Sauté the chops until golden brown on both sides, about 5 to 6 minutes per side, depending on the thickness of the chops.

Put the skillet in the hot oven to finish cooking the chops for about 12 to 14 minutes longer, depending on the thickness of the chops. When done, carefully remove the chops from the hot skillet to a dish; cover and keep warm while you prepare the sauce.

Carefully place the same hot skillet on the stove on medium-high heat, and add 2 pats of butter and stir until melted. Stir the flour into the chicken broth until dissolved; add to the skillet along with the herbs, the wine, and salt and pepper to taste. Stir and scrape the skillet with a wooden spoon to lift all the brown bits collected at the bottom of the skillet to add more flavor to the sauce. Cook and stir for about 6 to 7 minutes until the wine evaporates and the sauce starts to slightly thicken. Adjust the seasoning if needed.

Transfer the chops to a serving dish, spoon some of that delicious sauce on top, and serve at once with your favorite side dishes.

Perfect for a romantic dinner for 2!

Stuffed Pork Tenderloin

Filetto di Maiale Ripieno

2 pork tenderloins about 1 to 1-1/2 pounds each
1 package of pancetta, about 3 ounces
2 dried figs, coarsely chopped
4 to 6 ounces gorgonzola cheese
2 tablespoons flour (for dusting)
2 to 3 tablespoons extra-virgin olive oil
Salt and freshly ground black pepper to taste
Cooking twine for tying

Preheat oven to 400 degrees.

Have your butcher open up your tenderloins flat like a cutlet. Place your tenderloins open flat on a wooden board, and pound to make sure the meat is an even thickness. Heat an ovenproof large skillet to medium-high heat, and add the pancetta slices. Sauté the pancetta slightly for about 40 to 45 seconds, turning once, then turn the heat off.

Sprinkle both tenderloins with salt and pepper. Cover the surface of the tenderloins evenly with the pancetta. Sprinkle a few pieces of the chopped figs, and dot with the gorgonzola cheese evenly all over the top.

Roll the tenderloins tightly, jellyroll style, and tie with the twine at about 1 inch apart. Sprinkle the rolls all over with some flour. In the same skillet you used to sauté the pancetta, add 2 tablespoons of olive oil and turn the heat to medium. Add the rolled tenderloins and sauté all over for about 15 minutes, turning a few times until they reach a nice golden color all over.

When done, place the skillet in the heated oven to finish cooking the tenderloins. Cook for about 15 minutes more, or until the thermometer reaches 155 to 160 degrees. When done, carefully take the hot skillet out of the oven, put the tenderloins in a dish, cover with foil, and keep warm.

Sauce;
2 pats of butter
1 medium shallot, minced
3 sprigs parsley, leaves only chopped
3 sprigs thyme, leaves only minced
1-1/2 cups chicken broth
1/4 cup dry white wine
1 tablespoon flour
Salt and freshly ground black pepper

Place the same skillet that you cooked the tenderloins in on the stove, and turn the heat to medium. Add the butter and the minced shallot, and stir until the shallot is soft and translucent. Add the wine and continue to cook, scraping and stirring with a wooden spoon, in order to get all the bits gathered at the bottom of the skillet, about 2 to 3 minutes longer. Stir the flour into the chicken broth until dissolved, and add to the skillet along with half of the parsley and all of the thyme.

Continue to cook the sauce for about 6 to 8 more minutes or so, stirring often until the sauce slightly thickens. Adjust the seasoning if needed, then turn the heat off; cover and keep warm.

Transfer the tenderloins to a cutting board and remove the cooking twine. Cut the tenderloins into 1/2 inch slices. Transfer to a serving platter, spoon some of the sauce on top, and sprinkle with the remaining parsley for garnish.

Serve immediately with your favorite side dishes and the rest of the sauce to pass around at the table.

Delicious!

One of my favorite recipes!

Serves 6 to 8

Pork Chops with Fennel Sauce

Costolette di Maiale con Salsa di Finocchio

6 center-cut pork chops (bone in)
1/2 of a small can of tomato paste
2 tablespoons fennel seeds, slightly crushed
1 teaspoon whole fennel seeds for garnish
1 medium garlic clove, minced
1/4 cup flour for dusting
1-1/2 cups sweet Marsala wine
2 tablespoons Worcestershire sauce
2 tablespoons extra-virgin olive oil
1 tablespoon hot water
Salt and freshly ground black pepper to taste

Heat a large skillet on medium-high heat and add the olive oil. Wipe off any moisture on the chops with paper towels, and dust with flour. Place in the frying pan a few at a time. Lower the heat to medium, and sauté until golden on both side, about 5 to 6 minutes per side, or until the chops are cooked through. When done, take the chops out of the skillet, cover, and set aside.

In the same skillet, add the garlic and the crushed fennel seeds. Sauté for about 30 seconds. Dilute the half can of tomato paste with the water, add to the skillet and stir. Add the Marsala wine, the Worcestershire sauce, salt and freshly ground black pepper to taste and continue to cook, stirring until you achieve a smooth sauce, about 5 to 6 minutes.

Add the chops back in the skillet and turn them over a couple of times to make sure they soak up the sauce. Cook covered for about 2 to 3 minutes longer, until the chops are heated through. Transfer the chops to a serving dish. Pour all the sauce over the chops, and sprinkle the 1 teaspoon of the whole fennel seeds on top. Serve immediately with your favorite side dishes.

Serves 6.

Clelia's Easter Roasted Lamb

Arrosto d'Agnello di Pasqua alla Clelia

For the roast:
6 to 7 pound leg of lamb
12 medium garlic cloves, peeled and cut into slivers
6 rosemary sprigs
1/2 cup extra-virgin olive oil
1/2 cup red wine vinegar
1 cup good red wine
1 cup beef broth
4 pats butter
2 to 3 tablespoons flour
Salt and plenty of freshly ground black pepper

For the potatoes:
5 to 6 pounds red potatoes
12 to 14 cipolline (little Italian onions) or
7 to 8 medium yellow onions, cut into quarters
4 rosemary sprigs, minced
Salt and freshly ground black pepper

Heat oven to 350 degrees.

Trim fat off the lamb. Put it in a large bowl, pour the vinegar over it and massage it all over with your hands. When done, place the lamb in a large roasting pan, preferably of stainless steel, so that it is safe to place it back on the stove burners, to make the sauce later.

With the point of a sharp knife, make some incisions all around the roast, and insert some garlic slivers, some rosemary needles. Sprinkle the roast with salt, plenty of freshly ground black pepper, and a generous brush of olive oil all over.

Rinse the potatoes and dry well with paper towels. Cut into quarters and place them in a large bowl. Peel the onions and cut them into quarters as well. If using the cipolline, just peel, and leave them whole. (I prefer the cipolline.) Add the onions, rosemary, and the remaining garlic cloves to the bowl with the potatoes, and 1/4 cup of olive oil, some salt and freshly ground black pepper. Mix everything well to make sure the potatoes and onions are well coated with the olive oil and salt and pepper.

Place the potatoes and onions all around the roast. Place the roasting pan in the heated oven and cook the roast for about 1- 3/4 to 2 hours, or until the thermometer registers 160 degrees for medium rare or 170 to 175 degrees for medium well. Stir the potatoes and onions every 15 minutes or so to make sure they cook evenly all around and do not stick to the pan. Add a little more olive oil if they seem to stick.

When the roast is done, take it out of the pan onto a carving board. Cover with foil, and allow to rest. Stir and continue to cook the potatoes and onions 5 to 6 minutes longer to a nice golden color. Remove the potatoes and onions to a dish as well, and keep them warm and covered with foil.

In the meantime, start making the sauce. Place the same roasting pan over 2 burners on medium-heat. Add about 2 to 3 tablespoons of flour and 4 pats of butter. Start to heat and scrape the pan with a wooden spoon for 2 to 3 minutes or until the flour becomes golden brown. Add the wine, the beef broth, and salt and pepper to taste. Continue to cook and stir until the sauce becomes smooth and slightly thickened, about 5 to 6 minutes longer, then strain it into a bowl.

Slice the lamb into 1/4 inch slices, Transfer to a large serving platter, and place the potatoes and onions all around the roast. Spoon some sauce over the lamb and pour the rest into a gravy boat. Serve at once with more sauce to pass around at the table.

Buona Pasqua!

Serves 8 to 10.

Beef Braciolettine

Braciolettine di Manzo

12 slices of eye round roast thinly sliced
2 to 3 tablespoons extra virgin olive oil
12 slices of prosciutto cotto (ham)
1 packed cup of flat-leaf parsley, chopped
1 large garlic clove, minced

1-1/3 cups grated Pecorino Romano or Parmesan cheese
1 cup sweet Marsala wine
2 tablespoon Worcestershire sauce
2 tablespoons butter
Salt and freshly ground black pepper to taste
Toothpicks or twine for tying

Place the beef slices on a wooden board between two pieces of wax paper and pound with a mallet to even out the thickness. Line them up in a row on the wooden board and sprinkle with salt and pepper. Place one slice of ham on top of each slice of meat; top with a little sprinkle of garlic, a generous amount of parsley, a heaping tablespoon of grated Parmesan or Romano cheese, and a few drops of oil. Roll each slice tightly in order to make the braciolettine. Secure with toothpicks or cooking twine and set aside.

Add 2 tablespoons of olive oil to a large skillet and set it over a burner on medium-high heat. Put in a few braciolettine at a time. Do not crowd the braciolettine or they will not brown properly. Sauté lightly to a golden brown and then remove them from the skillet, cover, and set aside. Discard all but 1 tablespoon of the olive oil collected in the skillet. Add the butter, the Marsala wine, and the Worcestershire sauce. Scrape and stir the pan with a wooden spoon in order to collect all the bits left at the bottom of the pan.

Cook for about 2 to 3 minutes and then add the braciolettine back in the skillet. Continue to cook for about 2 to 3 minutes longer, so that the braciolettine will absorb all that nice sauce and are heated through as well.

Take the braciolettine out of the skillet; remove the cooking twine or toothpicks and arrange them on a serving platter. Continue to cook the sauce for about another minute or so. Adjust the seasoning if needed, stir and pour it over the braciolettine. Sprinkle some chopped parsley on top for garnish if you like, and serve at once.

Serves 6.

Pork Chops with Olives and Pine Nuts

Costolette di Maiale con Olive

4 center-cut pork chops
1/2 cup flour
12 green olives marinated with herbs
12 kalamata olives marinated with herbs
2 tablespoons pignoli (pine nuts)
1 cup good dry white wine
2 to 3 tablespoons extra-virgin olive oil
Salt and freshly ground black pepper to taste

Note: You can marinate olives with some dried herbs, such as oregano, basil, rosemary, fennel seeds, red pepper flakes, and 3 to 4 tablespoons of extra-virgin olive oil. Marinate overnight or for 3 to 4 hours for a real delicious sharp flavor. (You can also buy them in some markets.)

Heat the olive oil in a skillet on medium-high heat. Sprinkle some salt and pepper on each side of the chops. Dip each chop in the flour and shake the excess off. When the olive oil is hot, add the chops, lower the heat to medium, and start browning them. Cook each side for about 5 to 6 minutes or longer, depending on the thickness of the chops.

When cooked through, take them out of the pan, cover, and keep warm. Add the olives and the pignoli nuts to the same skillet, keeping the heat on medium, and sauté for 1 to 2 minutes. Add the wine and continue to cook for 2 to 3 minutes longer, just until the alcohol evaporates.

Transfer the chops back in the same skillet, and cook for about 1 to 2 minutes longer or until heated through. Transfer the chops to a serving platter and pour that delicious sauce over them. Serve immediately.

Serves 4.

Fish Recipes

Salmon with Pignoli Nuts

Salmone con Pignoli

2 pounds of salmon, skinless divided into 4 pieces
4 tablespoons pignoli nuts (pine nuts)
1/2 cup seasoned breadcrumbs
4 tablespoons extra-virgin olive oil
1 small garlic clove, minced or grated
Few sprigs of fresh herbs, leaves only, chopped (such as dill, thyme and parsley)
1 lemon
Salt and freshly ground black pepper to taste

Rinse the salmon with cold water and pat dry with paper towels. Brush with some oil, and sprinkle with salt and pepper to taste. In a small bowl, mix together the pignoli nuts, breadcrumbs, garlic, herbs, salt and pepper to taste. Press the herb mixture down with your hands over each piece on both sides to make sure the mixture sticks well to the fish.

Heat a large skillet on medium high heat and add 3 tablespoons of extra virgin olive oil. When the olive oil is hot, carefully place the salmon pieces down into the skillet, lower the heat to medium, and continue to cook the salmon pieces for about 1 to 2 minutes per side, depending on the thickness of the fish. When done, carefully remove to a serving dish, drizzle a little more olive oil on top, and a sprinkle of lemon juice. Garnish with a sprig of dill if you like, and serve at once.

Serves 4.

Cod with Three Peppers

Merluzzo con tre Peperoni

2 pounds of cod, one piece if possible
3 tablespoons extra virgin olive oil
1 large onion, chopped
1 large garlic clove, chopped
3 bell peppers, 1 each green, yellow, and red
About 12 white mushrooms, wiped cleaned and sliced

1/4 teaspoon cayenne pepper
2 tablespoons capers, rinsed and drained
1 cup kalamata olives, pitted
Salt and freshly ground black pepper to taste

Rinse and cut the peppers in half, scrape out the seeds, and cut into strips. Heat a skillet on medium-high heat and add 2 tablespoons of olive oil. Add the onion and sauté for about 2 minutes, stirring a few times until soft. Add the garlic and the bell peppers, and continue to cook and stir on medium-high heat, for about 5 more minutes or so. Then add the mushrooms, cayenne pepper, capers, olives, salt freshly ground black pepper to taste; continue to cook about 2 minutes longer.

Rinse and pat dry the cod with paper towels. Push the vegetables to the sides of the skillet, and place the cod in the middle of the skillet. Drizzle the remaining tablespoon of olive oil over the fish, lower the heat to medium, cover, and cook for about 8 to 10 minutes, or until the fish is cooked through, depending on the thickness of the fish.

When done, place all the vegetables in a serving platter, gently pick up the fish with a spatula, place it on top of the vegetables, and serve at once.

Serves 4.

Cod with Marinated Artichokes

Merluzzo con Carciofi sott' Olio

2 pounds of cod
3 tablespoons extra-virgin olive oil
1/3 cup seasoned breadcrumbs
Juice of 1 lemon and zest (organic)

1 (16 ounce) jar of marinated artichoke halves (juice drained and reserved)
Salt and pepper to taste
Chopped scallions (green part only) or chopped chives for garnish

Preheat oven to 375 degrees.

Brush 2 tablespoons of extra-virgin olive oil in a roasting pan. Rinse and pat dry the cod with paper towels. Add the fish and sprinkle it with the remaining tablespoon of olive oil, the lemon juice, breadcrumbs, lemon zest, and about 3 to 4 tablespoons of the reserved artichoke marinade. Arrange the artichokes all around the fish and place it in the oven.

Bake the fish for about 15 to 18 minutes, depending on the thickness of the fish or until cooked through. Divide the fish into 4 pieces and place each piece in a serving dish. Arrange some artichokes around the fish; garnish with a sprinkle of chives or scallions, and serve immediately.

Serves 4.

Halibut with Prosciutto

Halibut con Prosciutto

2 halibut steaks
1 small garlic clove, grated
1 tablespoon of extra virgin olive oil
1 pat of butter

8 sage leaves
4 slices prosciutto
1/2 cup dry white wine
1 pat butter
Salt and freshly ground black pepper to taste

Heat the oven to 400 degrees.

Rinse the halibut and pat dry with paper towels. Sprinkle it with just a little salt and pepper. Melt 1 pat of butter in a small pan, turn the heat off, and add the garlic. Brush the top of each piece of fish lightly with the flavored butter and garlic. Place 3 to 4 leaves of sage on top of each piece of fish. Wrap each piece of halibut with the prosciutto slices in order to cover just about the whole piece of fish as shown in the picture.

Heat 1 tablespoon of olive oil in an ovenproof skillet on medium-high heat. Add the halibut steaks top side down, and sauté until the prosciutto is lightly golden and slightly crispy, about 1 to 2 minutes. Carefully turn the fish over right side up with a spatula, and place the skillet in the oven.

Cook the fish for 10 to 12 minutes or until cooked through, depending on the thickness of the fish. Remove and place in a dish, cover, and keep warm. In the same skillet, add the wine, the other pat of butter, and a sprinkle of salt and pepper. Scrape the bottom of the pan with a wooden spoon to gather all the bits left in the pan. Cook just until the sauce slightly thickens and the wine evaporates; about 2 minutes or so.

Transfer the fish to a serving dish and pour the sauce over it. Garnish with some lemon slices and more sage leaves if you like.

Serve it with your favorite vegetable or with the broccolini as shown in the picture. Follow the recipe below.

Broccolini Recipe.

1 bunch broccolini
Juice and zest of 1 lemon
3 tablespoons extra virgin olive oil
Salt and pepper to taste

Rinse the broccolini in cold water. With a vegetable peeler, peal around the stems to make them more tender. Bring a medium size pan with about 1 quart of water and some salt to a rapid boil. Add the broccolini and cook for just about 2 to 3 minutes. Drain, and place in a serving dish. Wisk together the lemon juice, zest, olive oil, salt and pepper, and drizzle it over the broccolini just before serving.

Very delicious and a nice presentation!

Serves 2.

Fresh Tuna Balls over Spaghetti

Polpette di Tonno Fresco alla Siciliana con spaghetti

This recipe is very typical of the Sicilian cuisine:

1-1/2 pounds tuna fish steaks
3/4 cup golden raisins
1/2 cup dry white wine
1/2 cup pine nuts
1/4 cup mint leaves, coarsely chopped
1/4 cup flat parsley leaves, coarsely chopped
1/4 cup marjoram leaves, chopped
1/2 cup basil leaves, coarsely chopped
2 medium shallots, minced
1 medium garlic clove, minced
zest of 1 lemon (organic)
1/4 cup grated Pecorino Romano cheese plus more for sprinkling
2 eggs and 1 yolk
Salt and freshly ground black pepper to taste
1-1/4 cups Italian seasoned breadcrumbs
4 tablespoons extra-virgin olive oil
1 pound spaghetti pasta

Tomato sauce recipe:

2 tablespoons extra-virgin olive oil
4 garlic cloves, crushed
1/4 teaspoon crushed red pepper (optional but better)
3 (28-ounce) cans crushed tomatoes (good Italian quality)
Salt and freshly ground black pepper to taste

Heat a saucepan on medium-high heat with 2 tablespoons of extra-virgin olive oil, and add the garlic cloves. Sauté the garlic for about 30 to 35 seconds and then add 1/4 teaspoon of crushed red pepper flakes, the tomatoes, and salt and pepper.

Lower the heat to medium-low, and cook for about 1 hour uncovered, stirring occasionally. When done, turn the heat down to simmer, cover, and leave on the stove.

Preparation of tuna balls:

Place the raisins in a bowl, cover with the dry white wine, and soak for about 10 minutes to soften, and then squeeze out the wine.

In a food processor, add the raisins, pine nuts, mint, parsley, marjoram, basil, shallots, garlic, and salt and pepper. Process for about 30 seconds. Chop the tuna into chunks, and add to the processor as well. Pulsate just a few seconds until the tuna incorporates with the other ingredients. Take the mixture out of the processor and put it into a bowl; stir in 1/2 cup of the breadcrumbs, the cheese, the lemon zest, the 2 eggs and the yolk and mix all well.

At this point, start making the tuna balls by rolling some of the mixture in the palm of your hands very gently. The mixture will be soft and sticky. Moisten your hands with water to make shaping easier. Once done, roll each tuna ball lightly in the rest of the breadcrumbs.

Heat the olive oil in a large nonstick skillet over medium-heat. Add the tuna balls a few at a time and sauté until lightly golden on all sides, turning often. Place them in a dish lined with paper towels, as they get done. Once all done, turn the tomato sauce pan to medium-heat, When the sauce starts to gently bubble, add the tuna balls. Cover the pan, and cook for about 25 to 30 minutes, gently stirring occasionally.

Cook linguini according to package directions. When the pasta is cooked, strain it, and transfer to a serving bowl. Arrange the tuna balls on top of the pasta. Add some sauce over it, and garnish with some basil. Serve immediately with more sauce, and more grated cheese to pass around at the table if you like.

A great alternative to meat!

Makes about 2 dozen tuna balls depending on size.

Fresh Tuna with Herbs and Tomatoes

Tonno Fresco con Erbe e Pomodoro

4 fresh tuna fish steaks, about 1/2 pound each
Flour for dusting
4 tablespoons extra virgin olive oil
2 pounds cherry tomatoes cut in half
2 tablespoons capers, rinsed in cold water and drained
1/3 cup pitted kalamata olives, chopped
2 sprigs Italian flat parsley leaves, chopped
3 sprigs oregano leaves chopped, and 1 teaspoon dry oregano
3 medium garlic cloves, crushed,
1 small garlic clove, minced or grated
1/3 cup grated Pecorino Romano cheese
Salt and freshly ground black pepper to taste

Heat 2 tablespoons of olive oil on medium-heat. Add the 3 crushed garlic cloves, and sauté until lightly golden in color; 30 to 35 seconds. Add the tomatoes and some salt and pepper to taste. Cook on medium-low heat uncovered, for about 20 to 25 minutes stirring occasionally.

Rinse and pat dry the tuna with paper towels and season with salt and freshly ground black pepper on both sides, lightly dust with flour, and shake off excess. In a large skillet, heat 2 tablespoons of olive oil on medium-high heat. When the olive oil is hot, add the tuna steaks and sauté on both sides to a light golden color, about 1 to 2 minutes per side if you like it rare. When done, take them out of the skillet, cover and set aside.

Discard any olive oil left in the same skillet, and wipe it clean with paper towels. Add about 1 ladle of tomato sauce or enough to cover the bottom of the skillet. Place the tuna steaks on top of the sauce, sprinkle with the minced garlic, parsley, oregano, capers, olives, and about 3 tablespoons of the grated cheese. Spoon all the remaining sauce over the tuna. Add the rest of the cheese, cover, and cook just until the tuna is heated through.

Transfer to a serving dish, and serve immediately with your favorite side dish.

Try it, even if you don't like fish!

Serves 4.

Scallops with Rosemary

Capesante con Rosmarino

2 pounds of scallops
4 pats of butter
2 sprigs of fresh rosemary
2 cloves garlic
2 tablespoons hot sauce (optional)
1/4 cup flour
Salt and freshly ground black pepper to taste

Rinse scallops with cold water, and pat dry with paper towels. Sprinkle with some salt and pepper to taste. Dust with flour and shake off excess.

Heat a skillet on medium-high heat. Add the butter and garlic cloves and sauté the garlic until golden in color, about 30 to 35 seconds, then discard. Add the rosemary sprigs and the scallops. Cook, turning often until golden on all sides and cooked through, about 2 to 3 minutes.

When done, transfer the scallops to a serving dish, sprinkle some hot sauce over them if using, and add a sprig of rosemary for garnish. Serve immediately nice and hot with your favorite side dishes.

Serves 4.

Cod with Puttanesca Sauce

Merluzzo alla Puttanesca

2 pounds fresh cod (one piece and thick if possible)
6 tablespoons extra-virgin olive oil
1 medium shallot, minced
2 medium garlic cloves, minced
1/4 teaspoon red pepper flakes
4 anchovy filets in olive oil, drained
5 cups cherry tomatoes, cut in half
2 tablespoons capers, rinsed in cold water and drained
1 cup pitted kalamata olives, coarsely chopped
1/4 cup fresh oregano leaves, coarsely chopped
1/4 cup flat parsely leaves, coarsely chopped
1/2 cup basil leaves, coarsely chopped
reserve some sprigs of herbs for garnish

Heat the oven to 375 degrees.

Heat 2 tablespoons of olive oil in an ovenproof large skillet on medium-heat. Add the shallot and sauté just until soft. Add the garlic and continue to sauté and stir for 30 seconds longer. Put in the anchovies and stir until the anchovies just about disappear. Then add the tomatoes, capers, olives, and all the chopped herbs. Stir in the red pepper flakes, lower the heat to medium-low, and stir everything once again. Cook for about 10 to 12 minutes uncovered.

In the meantime rinse the cod with cold water, and dry with paper towels. Sprinkle with some salt and pepper, brush with some olive oil and place in the middle of the skillet with the sauce. Cover with foil and bake in the heated oven for about 15 minutes or so, depending on the thickness of the fish.

When done, take the foil off, arrange in a serving platter, garnish with the reserved herbs, and serve.

A little spicy but very tasty!

Serves 4.

Stuffed Filet of Sole

Filetti di Sogliola Imbottiti

6 filets of sole
1/2 pound of swordfish, cut into small cubes
1/4 cup cognac
1/3 cup breadcrumbs
1 small to medium onion, chopped
12 slices Fontina cheese
2 tablespoons fresh thyme leaves, minced
2 tablespoons fresh oregano leaves, minced
2 tablespoons fresh basil leaves, chopped
2 tablespoons fresh flat parsley leaves, chopped
4 to 5 tablespoons extra-virgin olive oil (more if needed)
Salt and freshly ground black pepper to taste
Cooking twine

Heat 2 tablespoons of olive oil in a medium size frying pan. Add the onion and sauté for about 5 to 7 minutes or until translucent and lightly golden. Add the swordfish, salt and pepper to taste, and a little more olive oil if needed. Stir and continue to sauté until the swordfish is no longer pink, about 1 to 2 more minutes. Add the cognac, turn the heat off and stir in the breadcrumbs, thyme, oregano, basil, parsley, and set aside.

Preheat oven to 375 degrees.

Rinse the fish filets with cold water and pat dry with paper towels. Line them up on a board with the narrow end facing you. Place 1 or 2 slices of the cheese on top of each filet. Then add 1 to 2 tablespoons of the swordfish stuffing on top, and start rolling the fish away from you, jellyroll style. Secure each roll with the cooking twine. Continue in the same manner with the rest of the fish filets.

Brush a roasting pan with about 2 tablespoons of olive oil. Add the fish rolls seam side down, and brush the top with olive oil and a sprinkle of freshly ground black pepper. Put the roasting pan in the heated oven, and roast the fish rolls for about 12 to 14 minutes. Check the time to make sure not to overcook them, or they will not hold together well.

In the meantime quickly start making the sauce.

1/2 cup extra-virgin olive oil
Juice and zest of 1 lemon (organic)
1 small garlic clove, minced or grated
2 tablespoons each of fresh thyme, oregano, basil, and parsley, (leaves only) finely chopped
2 to 3 tablespoons water
Salt and freshly ground black pepper to taste

In a small saucepan add the olive oil, lemon juice, lemon zest, garlic, herbs, the water, and salt and pepper. Beat everything with a fork until slightly thickened. Place on the stove on medium-heat, and heat just before it comes to a boil. Do not boil.

When the fish rolls are done, gently remove the twine from the fish rolls, making sure you do not breack them. Transfer to a serving platter, spoon some of the sauce over it, and serve at once, passing more sauce at the table.

Serves 6.

Shrimp Scampi

Gamberi con Aglio e Erbe

2 dozen extra-large shrimp, shelled, deveined, and with tail left on
1 tablespoon extra-virgin olive oil
6 tablespoons butter
4 large garlic cloves, finely minced
1/4 teaspoon red pepper flakes (more if desired)
1 cup Italian (flat) parsley leaves, coarsely chopped
Juice and zest of 1 lemon (organic)
Salt and freshly ground black pepper to taste

Heat the olive oil and butter in a skillet over medium heat. Add the garlic, red pepper flakes, stir and add the cleaned shrimp and some salt and freshly ground black pepper. Continue to stir for about 4 to 6 minutes, or until the shrimp becomes pink and cooked through.

Sprinkle the shrimp with the lemon juice, lemon zest, and the parsley. Adjust the seasoning if needed, and stir for a few more seconds. Transfer to a serving platter, garnish with some lemon slices or wedges, and serve immediately while nice and hot!

Serves 6 to 8.

Shrimp with Peppers and Polenta Wedges

Gamberi con Peperoni e Polenta

Note: If you like to serve the shrimp and peppers with the polenta wedges, make the polenta first (see polenta recipe below) or just serve the shrimp with the peppers—both ways are equally delicious!

Shrimp and peppers recipe:

4 peppers, 2 red, 1 green, and 1 yellow, sliced into strips
4 tablespoons extra-virgin olive oil
1 medium onion, chopped
2 garlic cloves, thinly sliced

12 to 14 extra-large shrimp
3 pats of butter
1/4 teaspoon red pepper flakes (optional)
Salt and freshly ground black pepper to taste

In a large skillet on medium-high heat, add 2 tablespoons of the olive oil and the onion. Sauté the onion until translucent and then add the garlic and continue to sauté, stirring for about 45 to 50 seconds or so. Put in the sliced peppers, stir all well, and continue to cook until the peppers are cooked but still crunchy, about 15 to 20 minutes. Add more olive oil if needed; sprinkle some salt, pepper and stir everything once again. Turn the heat off, cover and keep warm.

In a medium skillet on medium-heat, add the butter. When the butter has melted, add the shrimp, salt and pepper to taste, and the red pepper flakes if using. Cook and stir until the shrimp turns pink and cooked through, about 4 to 6 minutes or so. When done, add the shrimp to the peppers, turn the heat up on medium-high, and stir everything until just heated through. Transfer to a serving dish and serve at once.

Polenta recipe:

1 package (16 to 17 ounces) good Italian instant polenta
4 pats of butter
1/2 cup grated Parmesan cheese
plus 2 tablespoons for sprinkling
2 tablespoons fresh thyme, leaves only,
plus 1 tablespoon for sprinkling

Cook polenta according to package directions. (Buy a good Italian brand.)

Once the polenta is cooked, take it off the stove and stir in the following ingredients: 4 pats of butter, 1/2 cup Parmesan cheese, and about 2 tablespoons of fresh thyme leaves. Pour the polenta in a pie dish, smooth the top, and place in the refrigerator for about 1 hour or until the polenta becomes nice and firm.

When the polenta is firm, take it out of the refrigerator and cut it into wedges. Place the polenta wedges on a well-heated and oiled nonstick grill pan. Grill each wedge for about 2 minutes or so per side, until nice and golden in color. About 1 minute or so before removing the wedges from the grill pan, carefully sprinkle each wedge with some grated Parmesan cheese and a few thyme leaves. Do so while still hot so that the cheese will slightly melt.

Arrange them in the same platter with the shrimp and peppers as shown in the photo, if you like, and serve immediately.

This polenta recipe can also be served with any other entrée.

Serves 6 to 8.

Fresh Tuna Steaks Clelia Style

Tonno Fresco all Clelia

6 fresh tuna steaks of about 1/2 pound each
1/3 cup flour
3 tablespoons extra virgin olive oil
Salt and freshly ground black pepper

Rinse the tuna with cold water and dry well with paper towels. Sprinkle the tuna with salt and pepper on both sides. Dip very lightly in the flour on both sides and shake off the excess. Heat the olive oil in a large skillet on medium-high heat. Add the tuna steaks three at a time and cook for 1 to 2 minutes per side, depending on the thickness of the fish, and if you like it rare. When all the tuna steaks are cooked to your liking, turn the heat off, cover, and leave in the skillet, while you quickly prepare the sauce.

Sauce:

3 tablespoons small capers, rinsed, drained, and chopped
1 small garlic clove finely minced or grated
1 tablespoon smoked paprika
1/2 teaspoon salt
1 teaspoon freshly ground black pepper
1/3 cup extra-virgin olive oil

Mix everything well in a small pan, and place on the stove on medium-heat just long enough to warm. Transfer the tuna to a serving platter, spoon the sauce on each tuna steak, and serve immediately.

Serves 6.

Cod in White Wine and Lemon

Merluzzo al Vino Bianco e Limone

2 pounds cod, one thick piece if possible
5 tablespoons extra virgin olive oil
1/3 cup Italian seasoned breadcrumbs
1 lemon (juice only)
1 whole lemon sliced for garnish
1 clove garlic, thinly sliced
1/4 cup fresh Italian parsley leaves, chopped
1/4 cup dry white wine
Salt and freshly ground black pepper to taste

Preheat oven to 400 degrees.

Rinse the cod with cold water and pat dry with paper towels. Brush a roasting pan with some olive oil. Brush the fish with 1 tablespoon of olive oil, and a sprinkle of salt and pepper to taste. In a small bowl, add the wine, lemon juice, breadcrumbs, garlic, some parsley, 3 tablespoons of olive oil, and mix all well. Spread on top of the fish. Cover the fish loosely with foil, and bake in the preheated oven for about 10 minutes.

Remove the foil, and continue to cook for about 5 to 6 minutes longer or until the fish is cooked through and the breadcrumbs are a nice golden color. When done, carefully remove from the baking dish, and place on a serving platter. Drizzle it with a little more olive oil, garnish with the lemon slices, and a sprinkle of parsley.

Serve at once.

Serves 4.

Lemon Sole with Breadcrumbs and Lemon

Sogliola con Pane Grattugiato e Limone

8 lemon sole filets
5 tablespoons extra-virgin olive oil
1 teaspoon of lemon pepper
1 garlic clove, thinly sliced
1/2 cup Italian seasoned breadcrumbs
1/4 cup flat parsley leaves, finely chopped
Juice and zest of 1 lemon
Salt and pepper to taste

Heat oven to 375 degrees.

Rinse the filets with cold water and pat dry with paper towels. Brush a roasting pan with 1 tablespoon of olive oil. Add the filets to the roasting pan in a single layer. In a small bowl, add the lemon juice, lemon zest, lemon pepper, garlic, half of the parsley, the breadcrumbs, salt and pepper, and 3 tablespoons of olive oil. Mix all well, and spoon evenly over the fish.

Bake in the preheated oven for 12 to 14 minutes or so. When done, take the pan out of the oven, and carefully transfer the fish to a serving platter; drizzle the fish with one more tablespoon of olive oil, and a sprinkle of parsley. Serve immediately.

Serves 4

Stuffed Fresh Sardines

Sarde Fresche Ripiene

This is one of those dishes that brings back memories of growing up on the Bay of Naples where fresh fish, including sardines and anchovies was plentiful. Let me tell you..FRESH sardines and anchovies are nothing like the canned variety that most people are used to. If you can find the fresh sardines, I think you will enjoy this recipe. Try it!

8 fresh sardines
1-1/2 cups Italian seasoned breadcrumbs
1 large garlic clove, minced
1 tablespoon capers, rinsed, drained, and coarsely chopped
1 tablespoon raisins soaked in warm water and drained
2 tablespoons pignoli nuts, coarsley chopped (pine nuts)
1/2 cup grated Romano cheese
1/4 cup flat parsley leaves, chopped
2 eggs, beaten
2 tablespoons of water
6 to 7 tablespoons extra-virgin olive oil
1/3 cup flour to coat the fish
1 lemon
Salt and freshly ground black pepper to taste

Remove heads and insides from the sardines or have it done at the fish market.

Once the fish has been cleaned, rinse in cold water, gently dry with paper towels, and open it like a book without separating the fish. Carefully remove the spine and tail and any little bones very gently making sure the fish stays whole. It should come out very easily. Line them up flat in a row on a wooden board. Sprinkle a little salt and pepper on top of the fish, and set aside, while you make the stuffing.

In a medium size bowl, add the breadcrumbs, garlic, parsley, capers, raisins, pignoli, cheese, eggs, 3 tablespoons of olive oil, the water, and salt and pepper to taste.

Mix everything until well combined. Place about 1 to 2 tablespoons of the stuffing on top of each sardine, enough to cover the whole fish. Place another sardine on top to make a sandwich. Continue in the same manner with the rest of the sardines.

Heat a nonstick skillet on medium-high heat and add 3 tablespoons of olive oil. Dip each fish sandwich lightly in the flour on both sides and shake off the excess. Once the olive oil is hot, turn the heat down to medium and place the fish sandwiches in the skillet a few at a time. Continue to fry until golden on both sides, about 5 to 6 minutes per side, carefully turning once or twice to make sure they are evenly cooked.

Once the fish is done, transfer to a serving platter, drizzle a little more olive oil on top, and a generous sprinkle of lemon juice. Garnish with some herbs, and serve immediately nice and hot with any vegetables you like.

***Note** if the fish market does not have sardines on hand, usually they will be glad to order them for you.

Different, but worth trying!

Serves 4.

Vegetable/Side Dish Recipes

Eggplant Boats

Barchette di Melanzane

4 eggplants (preferably the same size)
1 large garlic clove, chopped
5 medium tomatoes, skinned, seeded, and chopped
3 tablespoons capers, rinsed in cold water and squeezed
1 cup pitted kalamata olives
1 cup basil leaves
1/2 cup parsley leaves
1/4 cup oregano leaves
1 tablespoon dried oregano
2 tablespoons pignoli nuts (pine nuts)
1/2 cup shredded Fontina cheese
5 to 6 tablespoons Italian seasoned breadcrumbs
1 cup extra-virgin olive oil
Salt and freshly ground black pepper

Heat the oven to 400 degrees.

Rinse the eggplants and dry with paper towels. Cut the top off each eggplant. Cut one whole eggplant with the skin on into cubes, place in a large bowl, and set aside. Cut the other three in half, lengthwise. Scoop out all the pulp from each half, leaving the shell about 1/4 inch throughout the whole eggplant.

Now you have six perfect shells. Chop the pulp into cubes as well, and add to the cubed eggplant, Put all the cubed eggplant in a large bowl, sprinkle with about 3 tablespoons of salt. Fill the bowl with enough cold water to cover the eggplants by 2 to 3 inches. Let soak for about 30 minutes or so, to draw out the bitter juices from the eggplant seeds. Drain, and dry well with paper towels, no need to rinse.

Brush the eggplant shells generously with olive oil inside and out. Sprinkle the inside of the shells with some salt and pepper. Place them on a cookie sheet lined with parchment paper, skin side down, and place under the broiler in the middle rack. Broil for about 15 to

20 minutes or until light golden in color. Check once or twice to make sure they do not burn. They should feel soft when inserted with a fork. When done, take them out of the broiler, and set aside to cool while you prepare the stuffing.

Heat a large skillet on medium-high heat, and add about 3 tablespoons of olive oil. When the oil is hot, add all the cubed eggplants to the skillet, stir, and put the cover on, but slightly off. Cook still on high-heat adding more olive oil if needed, stiring often.

When the eggplant is soft and a golden color all over, take the cover off, stir in the garlic, the fresh tomatoes, basil, parsley, fresh oregano, dried oregano, pignoli, capers, and olives. Stir everything thoroughly again, and continue to cook for about 10 more minutes until the eggplant is cooked through and all the ingredients have blended in thouroghly.

Stir in the breadcrumbs; taste and adjust the seasoning if needed. Turn the heat off and let cool for 5 minutes or so and then stir in the Fontina cheese. Mix all well again, and start filling each shell generously with the stuffing.

Once all the shells are filled, place the eggplant shells on a cookie sheet lined with parchment paper. Sprinkle just a little more Fontina cheese on top of each shell, and cook in the heated oven for about 15 minutes or so uncovered.

Cool slightly and place each eggplant shell on a nice large Romaine lettuce leaf for presentation. Drizzle a little olive oil on top of each eggplant and transfer to a serving platter. Serve immediately as an entrée or as a side dish.

I call them boats, because they resemble a little row boat.

Serves 6 to 8.

Eggplant Parmesan Neapolitan Style

Melanzane alla Parmigiana Napoletana

4 medium to large eggplants
1 cup extra virgin olive oil for brushing, more as needed
1 garlic clove, minced
2 tablespoons dried oregano
1/2 cup fresh parsley leaves, chopped
1/2 cup fresh basil leaves, chopped
1 cup grated Parmesan or Pecorino Romano cheese or mix half of each
2 large balls fresh mozzarella, thinly sliced

For marinara sauce:
4 large garlic cloves, crushed
2 tablespoons extra-virgin olive oil
2 (28-ounce) cans of chunky or crushed tomatoes (good Italian brand)
Salt and freshly ground black pepper
1/2 teaspoon red pepper flakes (optional but better)

Preheat oven to 350 degrees.

Start by making the Marinara sauce first.

In a medium saucepan on medium-high heat, sauté the garlic in the 2 tablespoons of olive oil for 45 to 50 seconds, or until light golden in color. Add the red pepper flakes if using, the tomatoes, and salt and pepper to taste. Lower the heat to medium, until the sauce starts to slightly bubble. Turn the heat down to medium-low and cook uncovered, for about 35 to 40 minutes stirring occasionally.

In the meantime, rinse and slice the eggplants about 1/4 inch thick leaving the skin on. Place the slices in a large bowl or pan with about 3 tablespoons of salt. Fill the bowl or pan with enough cold water, to cover the eggplants by 2 to 3 inches. Let the eggplants soak for about 30 minutes or so, to draw out the bitter juices from the eggplant seeds. Drain, and dry the slices with paper towels, no need to rinse.

Brush the slices with olive oil on both sides and place under the broiler or on a grill pan. Broil or grill until lightly golden on both sides, taking them out and placing them in a dish lined with paper towels as they get done. Once they are all done, cover, and set aside.

Take a 10 x 12 roasting pan and add about 1 to 2 ladles of tomato sauce; enough to cover the whole bottom of the pan. Top with a layer of eggplants, a light sprinkle of garlic, some parsley, basil, oregano, grated cheese, and a few slices of the mozzarella, followed by some more sauce.

Continue in the same manner with each layer, ending the top layer with the eggplant, some garlic, parsley, basil, oregano, a few slices of mozzarella, a little more tomato sauce, and a sprinkle of grated cheese. Bake in the hot oven for about 25 to 30 minutes or so, uncovered, until it starts bubbling and the mozzarella has slightly melted. Take it out of the oven and let rest for about 10 to 15 minutes before serving.

Note: You can also fry the eggplants in olive oil. I prefer broiling or grilling so it does not soak up a lot of oil.

Very light and tasty!

Serves 6 to 8.

Italian Vegetable Casserole

Casseruola di Verdure

2 medium zucchini squash, sliced
2 medium Italian eggplants, sliced
2 Portobello mushrooms, sliced
2 pounds baby spinach, rinsed and spun-dried
2 large potatoes, sliced
2 large yellow onions, sliced

6 large tomatoes, sliced
2 cups seasoned breadcrumbs
1 cup of grated Romano or Parmesan cheese
1 cup extra-virgin olive oil
1/4 cup dry oregano
Salt and freshly ground black pepper

Heat oven to 400 degrees.

Brush the bottom and sides of a 10 x 13 baking pan generously with the olive oil. Start by rinsing, scrubbing, and slicing the vegetables. Peel and slice the potatoes into about 1/4-inch rounds. Cut enough rounds to cover the bottom of the roasting pan. Slice the zucchini, eggplants, onions, tomatoes and the mushrooms into about 1/4-inch slices as well.

Now start assembling the vegetables in the prepared pan. Add a layer of potatoes. Top with a sprinkle of breadcrumbs, cheese, oregano, some spinach leaves, a good drizzle of olive oil, and a sprinkle of salt and freshly ground black pepper to taste.

Next, layer the eggplant slices, and top with a sprinkle of breadcrumbs; a sprinkle of cheese, oregano, spinach leaves, salt and pepper to taste, and a drizzle of olive oil, Continue in the same manner with each layer of vegetables; the onions, mushrooms, zucchini, tomatoes, and salt and pepper to taste until all the vegetables are used up.

End the top layer with the sliced tomatoes, a sprinkle of oregano, a light sprinkle of pepper, cheese and breadcrumbs, and a good drizzle of olive oil.

Place in the heated oven loosely covered with foil for about 1 hour or until the vegetables feel soft when inserted with a fork or knife. Take the foil off for the last 15 minutes of the cooking time. When cooked, take the pan out of the oven, and let it rest for about 15 minutes before serving.

Serves about 8 as a main course, with some hot ciabatta bread.

Asparagus with Goat Cheese

Asparagi con Formaggio di Capra

**1 bunch of asparagus
1/2 cup parsley leaves, coarsely chopped
1/3 cup marjoram leaves, coarsely chopped
1 garlic clove, minced
4 to 5 tablespoons olive oil
1 log of goat cheese, sliced about 1/4 inch thick
2 to 3 radishes, sliced, for garnish
Salt and pepper to taste**

Cut off the woody part of the asparagus. Peel the asparagus lightly all around with a vegetable peeler, and rinse in cold water.

Fill a medium pan with about 1 quart of salted water on medium-high heat. When the water starts to boil, add the asparagus, cover and cook for 2 minutes or so, depending on the thickness of the asparagus. Cook the asparagus just until lightly crunchy. Drain, run under cold water, and set aside.

In the meantime, slice the log of cheese and set aside. In a food processor, process the parsley, the marjoram, garlic, salt and pepper. Add in the olive oil while the processor is running. Stir and adjust the seasoning, if needed.

Arrange the asparagus on a serving dish, place the cheese slices across the top as shown in the picture. Drizzle the herb sauce on top, and garnish with some slices of radishes and a sprig of parsley to add color.

Serves 2 to 4

Butternut Cutlets

Cotolette di Zucca

2 long-neck butternut squash
2 eggs, beaten
1/2 cup flour
1 cup seasoned breadcrumbs
6 tablespoons extra-virgin olive oil

Preheat the oven to 350 degrees.

Choose a butternut squash with a long neck. Slice the neck part only into about 1/4 inch rounds. Save the rest for another time. Cut the skin off each slice, rinse with cold water, and dry with paper towels. Set out two flat dishes; one with flour, one with breadcrumbs, and a bowl with the beaten eggs.

Dip each slice first in the eggs, then flour, then egg again, and then breadcrumbs. Continue in the same manner until all done. Line a cookie sheet with parchment paper and brush some of the olive oil all over the paper. Put the squash rounds in a single layer on the cookie sheet and sprinkle generously with the olive oil all over. Place in the heated oven for about 15 minutes or until golden brown, and feel soft when inserting a toothpick or fork.

When done, arrange in a serving dish, and serve at once nice and hot!

Serves 4 to 6.

Green Beans with Rosemary

Fagiolini con Rosmarino

**1 and 1/2 pounds green beans
1/2 stick salted butter
2 sprigs rosemary, needles only, minced
1 rosemary sprig for garnish
Salt and freshly ground black pepper to taste**

Cut off the ends of the beans, rinse in cold water, and drain well. In a medium size pan set on medium-high heat, melt the butter. Add the beans, salt and pepper, and the minced rosemary needles. Turn the heat down to medium, cover and continue to cook. Cook for about 15 to 20 minutes or just until tender, stirring often. Adjust the seasoning if needed, transfer to a serving dish, sprinkle a little more freshly ground black pepper, and garnish with the rosemary sprig. Serve at once.

Serves 4 to 6.

Green Beans with Cannellini

Fagiolini Verdi con Cannellini

1 **pound green beans**
2 cans cannellini beans, rinsed and drained
2 large garlic cloves, thinly sliced
1/4 teaspoon red pepper flakes
4 to 5 tablespoons extra virgin olive oil
2 to 3 sprigs of Italian flat parsley leaves (optional)
Salt and freshly ground black pepper to taste

Cut the ends off the green beans, and rinse in cold water. Heat about 1 quart of salted water in a medium size saucepan, on medium-high heat. When it comes to a rapid boil, add the green beans and cook for about 15 minutes or so, or just until tender, and drain. Drain and rinse the two cans of cannellini beans as well.

Wipe the same saucepan with paper towels to make sure there is no water left in the pan. Heat the saucepan on medium-high heat and add 3 tablespoons of olive oil. Add the garlic, and sauté to a light golden color, about 30 to 35 seconds. Add the green beans, the cannellini beans, the red pepper flakes, and plenty of freshly ground black pepper. Stir everything well, and continue to cook on medium-high heat for about 8 to 10 more minutes until all the flavors are well combined, stirring often.

Transfer to a serving bowl, sprinkle with some more olive oil, and parsley if using, and serve at once.

Serves 6 to 8.

Eggplant Cutlets

Cotolette Di Melanzane

2 fresh eggplants
3 large eggs, beaten
1 cup Italian seasoned breadcrumbs
3 to 4 tablespoons olive oil (more if needed)
Salt and freshly ground black pepper to taste
2 to 3 sprigs basil leaves for garnish

Cut the top off the eggplants. Rinse with cold water and dry with paper towels. Slice into 1/4-inch slices with the peel on. Place the slices in a large bowl or pan with about 3 tablespoons of salt. Fill the bowl or pan with enough cold water to cover the eggplants by about 2 to 3 inches. Let soak for about 30 minutes or so, to draw out the bitter juices from the eggplant seeds. Drain and dry the slices well with paper towels, no need to rinse.

Heat about 3 tablespoons of olive oil on medium-high heat in a nonstick frying pan. Beat the eggs in a medium bowl with a little salt and pepper; put the breadcrumbs in a dish. Dip the eggplant slices first in the eggs and then in the breadcrumbs. Start frying the eggplants a few at a time in the hot olive oil. Place them in a dish lined with paper towels as they get done.

When all done, arrange them onto a serving dish; drizzle a little olive oil on top, some basil for garnish and serve nice and hot.

Serves 4 to 6.

Baked Stuffed Mushrooms

Funghi Ripieni

12 medium white mushrooms
3 pats of butter
1 tablespoon extra-virgin olive oil
1 large shallot, minced
2 scallions, light part only minced, save green part for garnish
1 medium garlic clove, minced
4 tablespoons grated Romano cheese
4 tablespoons shredded mozzarella
2 tablespoons ricotta
1 cup seasoned breadcrumbs
2 sprigs Italian parsley leaves finely chopped
1 tablespoon water (if needed)
Salt and freshly ground black pepper to taste

Preheat oven to 400 degrees.

Wipe the sand off the mushrooms with a damp towel, or quickly rinse with cold water and dry well with paper towels. Remove and mince the stems.

Heat a skillet on medium-high heat and add the butter and olive oil. Add the minced mushroom stems and sauté for 1 to 2 minutes. Add the shallot, garlic, scallions, parsley, and sauté everything for about 2 minutes longer.

Remove the skillet from the heat and add the breadcrumbs, grated cheese, ricotta, shredded mozzarella, salt and pepper, and a little water if needed. Mix everything well, and start stuffing the mushroom caps.

When done, place them stuffed side up, on a cookie sheet lined with parchment paper. Bake for about 11 to 12 minutes. Top with the chopped green scallions for garnish, and serve nice and hot!

Serves 4 to 6.

Stuffed Artichokes

Carciofi Ripiene

6 artichokes
1 cup Italian seasoned breadcrumbs
3/4 cup grated Pecorino Romano cheese
2 garlic cloves, minced plus 4 whole garlic cloves
1/2 cup Italian parsley leaves, chopped
10 tablespoons extra-virgin olive oil
Salt and pepper to taste
1 lemon

Cut the stems off each artichoke and peel with a vegetable peeler. Pull off the tough outer leaves of each artichoke and discard. Cut about a quarter off the top of each artichoke in order to get rid of all the thorns. Rinse in cold water and pat dry with paper towels. Rub all over with half a lemon, and put them upside down on a kitchen towel to drain.

Meanwhile, prepare the stuffing. Mix together the minced garlic, breadcrumbs, 1/2 cup of the grated cheese, chopped parsley, 5 tablespoons of olive oil, salt, and freshly ground black pepper. Loosen out the leaves of each artichoke by pushing down in the middle and out with your fingers in order to open them up. Place the stuffing between the leaves, and in the middle of each artichoke.

When done, put the artichokes in the pan standing up very snug together, so that they will not fall over. Add about 2 inches of water to the pan, some salt and pepper, the 4 whole garlic cloves, and the artichoke stems. Add a sprinkle of cheese and a drizzle of olive oil on top of each artichoke. Cover, and turn the heat to medium-high. As soon as the pan starts to boil, turn the heat down to medium-low, cover, and cook for about 1 hour or until tender.

Check often to make sure that there is always at least an inch of water at the bottom of the pan. Add a little more water if needed, and a sprinkle of salt.

Once the artichokes are cooked, transfer to a serving platter; spoon a little of the liquid left at the bottom of the pan into each artichoke, and serve along with the artichoke stems.

I just love them!

Serves 6.

Asparagus Wrapped in Prosciutto

Asparagi con prosciutto

1 bunch of asparagus
1/3 pound prosciutto, sliced thin
2 tablespoons extra-virgin olive oil
Salt and freshly ground black pepper to taste

Cut off the tough bottom part of the asparagus. Rinse in cold water, and using a vegetable peeler, peel off the rough parts, to make the stem more tender and attractive.

Bring 2 quarts of salted water to a rapid boil, and drop in the asparagus. Cook for about 2 to 3 minutes, depending on the thickness of the asparagus. Drain, and put in a bowl of ice water to stop the cooking. Drain and dry with paper towels. Place in a dish, and brush them with a little extra-virgin olive oil, a light sprinkle of salt, and freshly ground black pepper, in order to add more flavor.

Bundle together 2 or 3 asparagus and wrap the prosciutto around them. When all done, place them in a cookie sheet under the broiler and broil them for about 2 minutes, turning once. When the prosciutto starts to sizzle and is slightly golden, turn off the broiler and transfer them to a serving dish. Serve them with any meat or fish as a side dish.

Serves 4 to 6.

Stuffed Eggplant Rollups

Involtini di Melanzane

2 medium eggplants

Tomato sauce:
1 (28-ounce) can chunky or crushed tomatoes (good Italian brand)
3 large garlic cloves, crushed
2 tablespoons extra-virgin olive oil
1 small bunch fresh basil, leaves only, chopped
Salt and freshly ground black pepper to taste

Stuffing:
1 tablespoon extra-virgin olive oil
1-1/2 cups ricotta cheese
1/3 cup shredded mozzarella cheese
1 large shallot, minced
1 small garlic clove, minced
3/4 cup grated Parmesan cheese, (preferably Reggiano)
2 teaspoons dried oregano
6 to 8 fresh basil leaves, chopped
Salt and freshly ground black pepper to taste

Start by making the tomato sauce first.

Heat 2 tablespoons of olive oil in a medium saucepan on medium-high heat; add the garlic cloves. Sauté the garlic cloves slightly, about 35 to 45 seconds. Add the tomatoes, basil, salt and pepper, and stir. Turn the heat to medium-low, and cook uncovered for about 30 to 35 minutes, stirring occasionally.

In the meantime, rinse and dry the eggplants with paper towels. Cut the tops off and slice lengthwise with the skin on, about 1/4-inch thick. Place them in a large bowl or pan. Sprinkle with about 3 tablespoons of salt, and fill with enough cold water to cover the eggplants by 2 to 3 inches. Let soak for about 30 minutes or so, to draw out all the bitter juices from the eggplant seeds.

Drain and dry well with paper towels. No need to rinse. Put a grilling pan on the stove and turn the heat on high. When the pan is very hot, brush the eggplant slices with olive oil. Place on the grill pan for about 1 to 2 minutes per side. When done, put them in a dish lined with paper towels and allow them to cool while you prepare the stuffing.

Heat the oven to 350 degrees.

Heat 1 tablespoon of olive oil in a small skillet on medium-heat. Add the shallot and garlic and sauté, stirring for about 2 to 3 minutes or so, just until soft and fragrant. Turn the heat off, and cool.

In a medium bowl, add the ricotta, mozzarella, Parmesan cheese, the sautéd shallot and garlic, oregano, basil, salt and pepper to taste, and stir everything well. Line up the eggplant slices on a wooden board with the narrow side facing you. Spread about 2 to 3 tablespoons of the stuffing on each slice of eggplant and roll jelly-roll style away from you. Proceed in the same manner until all done.

In an 8 x 10 roasting pan, add about a ladle of the tomato sauce, enough to cover the bottom of the pan. Place all the eggplant rolls seam side down in the pan in a single layer. Top with 1 or 2 more ladles of sauce. Cover with foil, place in the heated oven for about 15 to 20 minutes or so. Take the foil off the last 8 minutes of the cooking time. Transfer to a serving platter, sprinkle some chopped basil on top (optional) and serve.

Serves 4 to 6.

Roasted Tomatoes with Mozzarella

Pomodori al Forno con Mozzarella

6 medium tomatoes
1 pre-sliced mozzarella package
3 tablespoons extra-virgin olive oil
1/2 cup flavored breadcrumbs
1/2 cup grated Romano cheese
6 basil leaves chopped

Salt and freshly ground black pepper to taste
1 teaspoon dried oregano

Herb Sauce:
1/3 cup extra-virgin olive oil
1/3 cup of mixed fresh herbs, basil, parsley, oregano, and thyme, leaves only, chopped
Salt and pepper to taste

Preheat oven to 400 degrees.

Slice about 1/4 inch off the top of the tomatoes, and remove the core and the seeds. Sprinkle the inside with salt and pepper to your taste. Mix together 1/2 cup of Romano cheese, 1/3 cup breadcrumbs, the chopped basil, and the 1 teaspoon of the dried oregano. Divide between each tomato, and add a good drizzle of olive oil over each. Place in a roasting pan and cook in the preheated oven for about 15 minutes or so, checking occasionally to make sure they remain firm.

While the tomatoes are cooking, heat a small nonstick skillet on medium-heat, and add 2 tablespoons of extra virgin olive oil. Press each slice of mozzarella into the remaining breadcrumbs on both sides and place in the hot skillet. Cook for just about 20 to 22 seconds per side, just until the breadcrumbs turn lightly golden. Take them out quickly as they get done, cover, and keep warm. Once the tomatoes are done, take them out of the oven, and quickly place a slice of the mozzarella on top while the tomatoes are still hot. Cover and keep warm.

In a food processor, combine the 1/3 cup of olive oil, the herbs, salt and pepper, and process just until the herbs are blended with the olive oil. Transfer the tomatoes to a serving dish, and spoon about 1 tablespoon of the herb sauce on top of the mozzarella, as shown in the picture and serve immediately. Great with any entrée!

Serves 6.

Artichoke Hearts with Kidney Beans

Cuori di carciofi con Fagioli Rossi

2 packages frozen artichoke hearts, defrosted
4 tablespoons extra-virgin olive oil
2 cans kidney beans, rinsed and drained
1 large garlic clove, minced
1/2 cup scallions, white and light green only, chopped
2 sprigs flat parsley, leaves chopped
1/3 cup freshly grated Parmesan cheese
Salt and freshly ground black pepper to taste

Heat the olive oil in a large skillet on medium-high heat. Pat dry the artichokes with paper towels. Add the artichokes to the skillet with salt and pepper to taste; cover and cook stirring often, until the artichokes are lightly golden and tender, about 10 to 12 minutes or so.

Add the garlic, scallions, and the parsley, and continue to cook and stir, with the heat still on high, for about 5 minutes longer. Add the drained beans, adjust the seasoning if needed, and continue to cook until the beans are heated through, about 3 to 4 minutes longer or so.

Turn the heat off, stir in the cheese, and transfer to a serving dish. Garnish with any herb of your choice.

Serve with your favorite entrée.

Serves 4

Spicy Artichoke Hearts

Carciofi Piccanti

2 packages frozen artichokes, defrosted
1 can diced fire-roasted tomatoes with green chilies
1/2 cup pitted kalamata olives
1 tablespoon capers, rinsed in cold water and drained
1 medium garlic clove, minced
2 tablespoons extra-virgin olive oil
2 sprigs flat parsley leaves, chopped
Salt and freshly ground black pepper

Heat a large skillet on medium-high heat and add the olive oil. Pat dry the artichokes and add to the skillet. Cook on medium-high heat for about 10 to 12 minutes until the artichokes are tender. Add the garlic and continue to sauté and stir for about 5 minutes longer. Add the tomatoes, olives, capers, salt and pepper to taste.

Continue to cook on medium-high heat uncovered, stirring often until the tomatoes are cooked through, and everything slightly thickens, about 10 to 12 minutes longer. Transfer to a serving dish, sprinkle with some parsley, and serve with your favorite meat, poultry, or fish.

Serves 4.

Stuffed Peppers

Peperoni Inbottiti

6 peppers 2 of each, yellow, orange, and red
2 cups Arborio rice
4 to 6 cups chicken broth (more if needed)
2 medium onions, chopped
2 garlic cloves, minced
1 celery stalk, chopped
1 medium carrot, chopped
2 tablespoons capers, rinsed and drained
1/2 cup sun-dried tomatoes in olive oil, drained, and coarsely chopped
1/2 cup pitted kalamata olives, coarsely chopped
1/4 cup pine nuts (pignoli)
2 pats butter
3 tablespoons extra-virgin olive oil
1 cup provolone cheese cut into small cubes
Salt and freshly ground black pepper

Preheat oven to 400 degrees.

Rinse the peppers and dry with paper towels. Cut the tops off about 3/4 inch down, and save the tops for garnish. Remove the seeds and pith gently from inside the peppers, making sure not to pierce them, and set aside.

Heat 1 tablespoon of olive oil, and 1 pat of butter in a saucepan, on medium-high-heat. Add 1 of the onions and sauté until soft and light in color. Add the rice to the same pan and toast and stir for about 1 minute or so. Add 4 cups of chicken broth and cover the pan. Once the pan starts boiling, turn the heat down to medium-low and cook for about 15 minutes, adding a little more broth if needed. Cook just until tender, adjust seasoning if needed, turn the heat off and set aside.

In a medium size skillet, heat 2 tablespoons of olive oil, and 1 pat of butter on medium-high heat. Sauté the remaining onion until soft. Add the garlic, celery, carrot, olives, pine nuts, and sun-dried tomatoes, and cook until everything is slightly soft. Turn the heat off and add the provolone cubes. Pour everything into the cooked rice, stir and set aside.

Sprinkle some salt and pepper inside the peppers. Stuff the peppers with the rice mixture and place in a roasting pan standing up. Brush the little tops with some olive oil, and add to the roasting pan as well. Sprinkle some olive oil on top of each pepper, cover with foil, and cook for about 20 to 25 minutes, depending on the size of the peppers. Remove the foil the last 5 to 6 minutes of the cooking time.

When done, remove from the oven. Cool slightly and transfer to a serving platter. Garnish with the pepper tops as shown in the picture.

Serves 6.

Artichoke Hearts Parmesan

Carciofi alla Parmigiana

4 packages frozen artichoke hearts, defrosted
1 large garlic clove, minced
2 tablespoons dried oregano
1 cup freshly grated Parmesan cheese
1 pound fresh mozzarella, sliced thin
1 cup fresh basil leaves, torn

1/2 cup flat parsley leaves, coarsly chopped
3 eggs beaten
1-1/2 cups Italian flavored breadcrumbs
1/2 cup extra-virgin olive oil
Salt and freshly ground black pepper

Start by making the sauce first.

4 large garlic cloves, crushed
2 tablespoons extra-virgin olive oil
2 (28-ounce) cans of chunky or crushed tomatoes (good Italian brand)

Salt and freshly ground black pepper
1/2 teaspoon red pepper flakes (optional but better)

In a medium saucepan on medium-high heat, sauté the garlic in the 2 tablespoons of olive oil for 45 to 50 seconds, or until light golden in color. Add the red pepper flakes if using, tomatoes, salt and pepper to taste. Lower the heat to medium until the sauce starts to slightly bubble, then turn the heat down to medium-low, and cook uncovered,for about 35 to 40 minutes, stirring occasionally to make sure the sauce does not stick.

Once you make the sauce, keep it on simmer while you prepare the artichokes. Pat dry the artichokes well with paper towels. Beat the eggs and some salt and pepper in a large bowl, and place the breadcrumbs in a flat dish. Dip some of the artichokes first in the eggs and then in the breadcrumbs. Do this in batches.

Heat a nonstick skillet on medium-high heat and add the olive oil. Once the olive oil is hot, start browning the artichokes in batches, and sauté to a golden brown. Put them in a dish lined with paper towels as they get done, and set aside.

Heat the oven to 375 degrees.

In a 9 x 11 roasting pan, add about 1 ladle of the marinara sauce, or enough to cover the bottom of the pan. Spread half of the artichokes evenly in one layer. Sprinkle the top with some minced garlic, oregano, basil, parsley and Parmesan cheese. Add some mozzarella slices, and spread another ladle of sauce. Top with the rest of the artichokes, the minced garlic, oregano, basil, parsley Parmesan cheese, mozzarella slices, and more tomato sauce.

Put the roasting pan in the oven loosely covered with foil, and cook for about 25 to 30 minutes. Uncover for the last 10 minutes of the cooking time. When done, cover them loosely with foil and let rest for about 15 minutes. Serve with a salad and some nice crusty hot bread if using as a main course, or as a side dish with any meat or chicken.

Serves about 6 as a main course

Neapolitan Potato Pie

Gatto'

6 large potatoes
6 large eggs
4 tablespoons extra-virgin olive oil
1/2 cup grated Pecorino Romano cheese
8 ounces mozzarella, cubed
6 ounces provolone cheese, cubed
1/4 pound prosciutto, chopped
8 ounces sopressata, cubed

1/2 cup fresh herbs, such as thyme and marjoram leaves, chopped
1 teaspoon dried oregano
1/2 cup seasoned breadcrumbs
1/4 teaspoon red pepper flakes (optional)

Heat the oven to 375 degrees.

Scrub and rinse the potatoes and place in a pan with skin on. Add enough water to cover the potatoes by 2 to 3 inches. Boil until soft when pierced with a fork. When just cool enough to handle, peel the skin off each potato, and place each one in a ricer. Squeeze all the potatoes into a large bowl. When done, sprinkle some salt, freshly ground black pepper, 2 tablespoons of the olive oil, and mix everything well. Start adding the eggs one at a time, mixing well with each one. Then add all the other ingredients, except breadcrumbs, and mix thoroughly until all the ingredients are well incorporated. Adjust the seasoning to your taste and put aside.

Brush the bottom and sides of a 10 or 12 inch pie dish with some olive oil. Add the breadcrumbs, and coat the bottom and sides of the pie dish completely with the breadcrumbs. Add the potato mixture and spread evenly into the pie dish. Sprinkle the top lightly with more breadcrumbs, the red pepper flakes if using, the oregano, and a generous drizzle of olive oil.

Bake for about 45 to 50 minutes or so uncovered, until the top looks nice and golden. When done, take it out of the oven, and let rest loosely covered for about 15 to 20 minutes before serving.

Serves 6 to 8 and can be served as a main dish or as a side dish.

Dessert Recipes

Growing up in Italy, sweets were not something that we had that often.

We usually ended our meals with fresh fruits and nuts. In Naples, we were blessed with a variety of delicious fruits. One of my favorites, among others, was a fruit called "nespole" and you could only get it for a very short time in the spring. Sweets were mostly for holidays and were usually bought at the local baker. Sfogliatelle, cannoli, baba,' were among my favorites. Since I have lived here, in the United States, I have come to enjoy making my own homemade sweets. The recipes in this chapter are some of my favorites, both old recipes and new ones.

A Bakery on Capri

Clelia's Cannoli

Cannoli a Modo Mio

12 Cannoli Shells, (18 if using small forms)

(Note: If you don't want to make the cannoli shells yourself, buy them already made and skip down to the filling recipes.)

How to make your own cannoli shells:

You will need cannoli forms. These can be found in any store that sells specialty kitchen items or online.

**2 cups flour
1/2 stick unsalted butter
1 pinch salt
1/3 cup dry white wine or Marsala wine
2 cups canola oil, (for deep frying)**

In a food processor, add the flour, salt and butter, and process just enough to mix, then add the wine and continue to process just until the dough comes together. Roll the dough into a ball; wrap it in cling wrap, and refrigerate for about 1 hour.

When ready, cut the ball of dough in half, and wrap the other half with cling wrap. Roll the dough until very thin, about 1/8 of an inch or so. Cut a disk about 3 to 4 inches in diameter using a cookie cutter or a glass or cup turned upside down. Wrap the dough disk around the cannoli form, and seal by wetting the ends with a little egg white. Do not get any egg white on the form; or it will make it difficult to remove once they are done. Continue with the other half of the dough in the same manner.

In a medium size heavy deep (5-6 inches) saucepan, add about 2 inches of canola oil, and heat until a deep frying thermometer reaches between 300 and 325 F. Very carefully, lower the cannoli into the hot oil by holding it with tongs. Cook only for about 1 minute or just until light golden in color. Take it out with the tongs very carefully, and place in a dish lined with paper towels. Continue in the same manner until all are done. When just cool enough to handle, gently twist the form and pull it out of the shell. Cool completely before filling.

Ricotta filling:

1 cup ricotta
1/4 cup powdered sugar, sifted
2 teaspoons vanilla

Garnish:

1 cup miniature semisweet choccolate chips
chopped pistachio nuts, walnuts, hazelnuts, or sprinkles, (as you prefer)

Mix all ingredients well, reserving 1/4 cup of the chocolate chips to garnish each end of the cannoli. When the cannoli shells are completely cool, fill them by using a pastry bag or a small spoon. Dip each cannoli end either in the reserved chocolate chips, the chopped pistachio nuts, or sprinkles; whatever you chose.

Custard filling:

1-1/3 cups whole milk
4 egg yolks
1/3 cup sugar
2 tablespoons cornstarch

2 tablespoons flour
2 teaspoons vanilla
Juice of 1/2 lemon

Heat the milk in a double boiler. In a mixing bowl, beat the egg yolks, sugar, cornstarch, and flour. Beat until smooth. Gradually add 1/3 of the hot milk into the egg mixture, and continue to beat until well combined. Add the whole mixture to the 1 cup of milk left in the double boiler and continue to whisk until the mixture thickens.

At this point, add the vanilla and the juice of the lemon to make sure the custard is nice and smooth and does not curdle. (Lemon helps custard not to curdle, and it also adds flavor.) Continue to stir to a nice smooth cream. Stir for about 1 to 2 more minutes, then take it out of the pan and put it into a bowl. Refrigerate until completely cool and thick. Once thick and cool, put it into a pastry bag and fill the cannoli shells.

Chocolate custard filling:

Follow the custard recipe but before refrigerating the custard add 1 or 2 packets of pre-melted bitter chocolate, and mix until well incorporated with the custard. Mix until you achieve a nice creamy consistency. Refrigerate until completely cool and thick. Put it into a pastry bag and fill the cannoli. Try a few with each filling if you like. All equally delicious!

Makes about 12 to 18 cannoli (if using small cannoli forms).

Note: Always fill the cannoli shells, just before serving or they will get soggy!

Italian Dessert Pizza

Pizza con Cioccolata all Nocciola

**1 pound pizza dough
1 cup Nutella
1/2 cup grated white chocolate
1/2 pound strawberries, sliced
4 kiwi sliced**

**1/2 cup whole walnuts
2 tablespoons each of green sprinkles, red sprinkles, and grated white chocolate, in order to make the Italian flag in the middle of the pizza.**

Preheat oven to 500 degrees.

Spread the dough in a large pizza tray and puncture all over with a fork. Place on the lowest rack of the oven, and bake for about 12 to 15 minutes or until golden.

Take it out of the oven, and carefully spread the Nutella all over while still hot. Sprinkle with the white chocolate and nuts. Add the sliced strawberries and the kiwi leaving some space in the middle so that you can make the Italian flag.

Pour a line of green sprinkles of about 1 inch wide and 3 inches long in the middle of the pizza, and then another line of the grated white chocolate right next to the green; another line of the red sprinkles right next to the white, in order to form the Italian flag as shown in the picture.

Put it back in the oven and cook for about 1 to 2 more minutes. When done, take it out of the oven, and let rest for about 6 to 8 minutes before slicing.

Fun to do with your children!

Serves 8 to 10.

Pine Nut Cookies

Biscotti con Pignoli

1-1/4 cups pine nuts (pignoli)
7 ounce tube of almond paste
1/2 cup sugar
1/4 teaspoon salt
2 egg whites
1 teaspoon vanilla extract
1/4 cup flour

Preheat oven to 325 degrees.

In a food processor, add 1/4 cup of the pignoli nuts and blend. Add the whole tube of almond paste along with the sugar and salt and continue processing. Add the egg whites one at a time, the vanilla, and the flour. Process everything together, making sure it is all well combined.

Line a cookie sheet with parchment paper. Take a spoonful of the very sticky batter and place on the cookie sheet about 1 to 1 1/2 inches apart until all the batter is used. Now top each cookie with enough pignoli nuts to just about cover the whole cookie. pressing down lightly with your fingers. Place the cookie sheet in the oven and cook until lightly golden, but for not more than 10 minutes. Cool and serve.

Makes about 1-1/2 dozen cookies.

Tiramisu' Clelia Style

Tiramisu' alla Clelia

16 ounces mascarpone cheese
3 tablespoons coffee liqueur
1 teaspoon vanilla extract
1/2 cup powdered sugar
1/2 teaspoon salt
4 squares semi-sweet Baker's chocolate, grated
1 cup whipping cream, whipped stiff

4 to 5 tablespoons instant espresso coffee, stirred in 3 cups lukewarm water
1 teaspoon vanilla extract
3/4 cup coffee liqueur
3 to 4 dozen savoiardi cookies (lady fingers)
Unsweetened cocoa powder for sprinkling the top

In a medium size bowl, whip the cream with an electric mixer until very stiff, cover and refrigirate.

In a large bowl, add and mix together the mascarpone cheese, 3 tablespoons coffee liqueur, vanilla, sugar, salt, and the grated chocolate squares. Mix everything well with an electric mixer until well combined. Fold the whipped cream into the cheese mixture a few spoonfuls at a time. When done, cover and refrigerate.

In a medium size bowl, stir the espresso coffee into the water, then add the vanilla, and the coffee liqueur.

In a 9 x 13 pan, start assembling the tiramisu'. Dip each savoiardi cookie into the coffee mixture, and start layering the bottom of the pan until it is completely covered. Top with enough cheese mixture to cover all the cookies. Continue in the same manner with the next layer. End the top layer with the remaining cheese mixture. Sprinkle the unsweetened cocoa powder generously all over the top, cover with plastic wrap, and refrigerate for several hours, or even better overnight.

Serves 10 to 12 or more. (This recipe is definitely for a large crowd.)

Ricotta Cream Pie

Crostata di Ricotta Panna e Cioccolata

Make your own 9 to 10 inch pie crust or make a graham cracker crumb crust by following the directions on the graham cracker box.

Make sure the pie crust is well chilled before putting in the filling.

Filling:
1 pound ricotta cheese, well drained
3/4 cup sugar
1 teaspoon pure almond extract
1 cup chopped almonds
1/2 cup semisweet chocolate chunks or chips
1-1/4 cups heavy cream, whipped stiff

Combine ricotta, sugar, and almond extract in a mixing bowl. Mix well and chill for about 1 hour. Fold the almonds and the chocolate chunks or chips into the ricotta mixture. Do not over stir. Whip the cream until very stiff. Fold it into the ricotta mixture with a spatula, a few large spoonfuls at a time.

When done, spoon it all into the chilled crust and smooth the top. Chill several hours or overnight. Garnish the top with chopped almonds and chocolate shavings before serving.

The same ricotta filling can be used to fill cannoli shells as well.

Serves 6 to 8.

Ricotta Pie with Gran Gala Liqueur

Crostata di Ricotta con Gran Gala

2 Crust pie:

2-2/3 cups flour
1 teaspoon salt
1 cup shortening
2 tablespoons powdered sugar
1 organic lemon, zest only, grated
1 teaspoon pure vanilla extract
7 to 8 tablespoons cold water

Mix flour, salt, sugar, vanilla, and lemon zest. Gradually cut in the shortening thoroughly. Sprinkle in the water, 1 tablespoon at a time, mixing with a fork until it all comes together. Form into a ball, wrap in cling wrap, and set aside while you prepare the filling.

Filling:

1-1/3 cups ricotta cheese, well drained
3 egg yolks
2 tablespoons honey
2 tablespoons Gran Gala, an Italian orange liqueur, (or Grand Marnier)
3 tablespoons golden raisins, softened in water and squeezed thoroughly
2 tablespoons candied orange
1/2 cup sugar

In a medium bowl add the ricotta, egg yolks, and sugar, and mix well. Then add the honey, candied orange, Gran Gala liqueur, and raisins. Mix everything together well with a hand mixer on medium speed or a fork; set aside while you prepare the pie shell.

Preheat the oven to 400 degrees.

Divide the dough in half and wrap one half in cling wrap. Roll out the bottom crust dough into a 12-inch disk, and place it in the pie plate leaving 1-inch overhang. Pour the filling into the pastry lined pie plate and put it aside. Roll out the other dough half into a 12 inch disk as well, and cut it into 1/2 inch wide strips.

Place 5 to 7 strips across the filling in the pie pan. Lay the second half of the strips diagonally across the first strips. Fold trimmed edge of lower crust over ends of the strips. Seal by pressing a fork all around the edge of the pie plate.

Place it in the oven and cook for about 35 to 40 minutes, or until the filling is set and the pastry is golden in color. Cool thoroughly and refrigerate for several hours or even better overnight.

Serves 8 to 10.

Stuffed Apples

Mele Imbottite

4 Gala or Granny Smith apples
1/3 cup raisins
1/4 cup amaretto liqueur
1/4 cup roasted pecans, chopped
1/4 cup walnuts, chopped
1/4 cup pine nuts (pignoli)
2 cups panettone, (Italian swet bread) cubed, or any sweet bread of your choice
1/3 cup heavy cream
1/4 cup semisweet miniature chocolate chips
4 semisweet chocolate squares, melted
1/2 stick sweet butter

Preheat the oven to 375 degrees.

Soak the raisins in the liqueur and set aside. Cut the top of the apples about an inch down and save the lids. Hollow out the apples, leaving about a 1/4-inch border all around. Squeeze the liqueur out of the raisins and add to a medium bowl, mix together the liqueur the raisins, pecans, walnuts, pine nuts, panettone, cream, and the miniature chocolate chips.

Mix everything together well and start stuffing the apples. When done, place the apples in a roasting pan along with the lids and cook in the preheated oven for about 35 to 40 minutes, or until the apples are tender enough to easily pierce with the point of a knife or a fork. We want the apples to be slightly firm so that they can hold their shape. When done, take them out of the oven, cover loosely, and set aside.

Place a double boiler on the stove with enough water to come to about 2 inches under the top pan, making sure the bottom of the top pan does not touch the water. Melt the butter in the pan and add the chocolate squares, stirring until the squares are melted to a smooth consistency.

Divide the melted chocolate among four dishes. Swirl the chocolate around each dish to form a pool. Place each apple in the middle of the dish, and place the lid on top of the apples slightly off, as shown in the picture, and serve.

A nice presentation!

Serves 4

Strufoli

Strufoli

2 cups all-purpose flour
4 eggs plus 1 yolk
1 organic lemon, zest only, grated
1 organic orange, zest only, grated
2 tablespoons butter, room temperature
1/4 teaspoon salt
6 tablespoons light olive oil or vegetable oil
1/4 cup each of candied citrus, orange, and lemon
1/2 cup honey
4 tablespoons sugar
1 teaspoon water, if needed
2 tablespoons sprinkles
1 cup red and green candied cherries for garnish

Mix the flour, orange and lemon zest, salt, and butter until well incorporated. Add the eggs one at a time, mixing well, and then the yolk. Once everything is mixed, turn the dough onto a floured wooden board, and lightly knead, adding more flour if needed. Dough should be slightly sticky. Take about 1 teaspoon full of dough in your hands and roll it into the size of a marble until all the dough is used.

In a medium size saucepan, heat the oil on high heat 300 to 325 degrees. When the oil is hot, start adding the little balls a few at a time and cook for 25 to 30 seconds or just until they are light golden in color. Place in a dish lined with paper towels as they get done and set aside.

Heat another medium size saucepan on medium-low heat, add the 1/2 cup honey and 4 tablespoons of sugar, stirring until the sugar melts and the honey starts foaming. Turn the heat to simmer and add about 1 teaspoon of water if too thick. Add all the candied citrus, orange, and lemon and keep cooking, stirring until the honey and sugar become clear.

Add the strufoli to the honey mixture, and stir until the honey is well combined with the strufoli. Cool slightly, place on a wooden board, and with your hands, shape it in the form of a wreath as shown in the picture. Carefully transfer to a serving dish, and garnish with some sprinkles, and a few red and green candied cherries on each side of the wreath, if you like. Eat it like sticky popcorn.

Nectarines with Amaretto and Pecans

Nettarine con Amaretto e Pecans

2 large nectarines
1 teaspoon brown sugar
1/4 cup pecans
2 pats of sweet butter
4 tablespoons amaretto liqueur

Heat a small skillet on medium heat and add the butter. Slice the nectarines and add to the skillet. Add the sugar and the pecans and sauté for about 1 to 2 minutes or so. Add the amaretto. and continue to stir for 1 more minute or so, until the alchohol evaporates, and everything is well coated and thickened. Cool slightly, divide between 2 dessert cups or glasses, and serve with a scoop of vanilla ice cream, a dollop of whipped cream, or just as is.

Serves 2.

Nectarines or Peaches in Wine

Nettarine o Pesche al Vino

This is a very typical and simple dessert in Southern Italy that men, especially, enjoy. After a Sunday dinner, when a pastry or sweet would be too heavy, this would be what you would serve, as well as a variety of fresh fruits and nuts.

One of my father's favorite desserts.

2 nectarines or peaches
red or white wine, or sweet Marsala wine

Slice either the nectarines or peaches, and divide between 2 serving cups or glasses. Fill the cups or glasses with any of the wines you prefer, and serve.

Refreshing and quick!

Serves 2.

Stuffed Pizzelle

Pizzelle Ripiene

18 pizzelle, vanilla or choccolate flavor
15 to 16 ounces ricotta cheese
8 ounces mascarpone cheese
1/2 cup powdered sugar
1-1/2 teaspoons pure vanilla extract
2 tablespoons Gran Gala or Grand Marnier liqueur
1- 1/2 cups heavy cream, whipped stiff
3 squares semisweet chocolate, grated
1/4 cup semisweet miniature chocolate chips
zest of one organic orange, grated
1/2 cup sliced almonds
16 ounces vanilla ice cream

In a bowl, mix together well, the ricotta, mascarpone, powdered sugar, chocolate chips, vanilla, liqueur, and orange zest. When everything is well blended, put the bowl in the refrigerator and cool for about 2 hours so that the mixture will get nice and cold.

When the mixture is ready, start assembling the pizzelle in 6 individual dishes. Place a pizzella in the middle of a dish, add a dollop of the cheese mixture, a sprinkle of almonds, and a sprinkle of the grated choccolate. Place another pizzella on top, and press down gently. Add another dollop of the cheese mixture, a sprinkle of almonds, and a sprinkle of choccolate. Top with another pizzella, and add a dolllop of whipped cream, ice cream, or both if you like; a sprinkle of the grated chocolate, and some sliced almonds.

Continue with the rest of the pizzelle in the same manner. Garnish the individual dishes with a few pieces of dried fruits and nuts if you like. Fun to make together!

Makes 6 individual servings

Conversion/Metric Equivalents

The recipes in this cookbook use standard US measurements such as pounds, cups, tablespoons, teaspoons, Fahrenheit, etc. If you use the metric system, this chart will help convert these recipes. These conversions are approximate so users may want to make any adjustments they like.

USA	Metric
1/4 teaspoon	1.25 milliliters
1/2 teaspoon	2.5 milliliters
1 teaspoon	5 milliliters
1 tablespoon	15 milliliters
1/4 cup	60 milliliters
1/3 cup	80 milliliters
1//2 cup	120 milliliters
1 cup	240 milliliters
1 pint or 2 cups	480 milliliters
1 quart or 4 cups	960 milliliters
1 gallon or 4 quarts	3.84 liters
1 liquid ounce	30 milliliters
1 dry ounce	28 grams
1 pound	454 grams
2.2 pounds	1 kilogram
1/2 inch	12 milliliters
1 inch	2.5 centimeters

Oven Settings

USA Fahrenheit (F)	Celsius (C)	Gas
250	120	1/2
275	140	1
300	150	2
325	160	3
350	180	4
375	190	5
400	200	6
425	220	7
450	230	8
475	240	9
500	260	10

Recipe Index

Arancini, 17
Artichoke Hearts Parmesan, 158
Artichoke Hearts with Kidney Beans, 154
Asparagus with Goat Cheese, 142
Asparagus Wrapped in Prosciutto, 150
Baked Rigatoni with Seafood and Cognac, 47
Baked Stuffed Mushrooms, 147
Beef Braciolettine, 111
Beef Rollups, 97
Bow Tie Pasta with Olive Pesto, 61
Bow Tie Pasta with Portobello Mushrooms, 49
Bruschetta, 9
Butternut Cutlets, 143

Chicken Breasts with Tuna Sauce, 89
Chicken Cacciatore, 84
Chicken Cutlets with Dried Apricots and Vermouth, 80
Chicken Cutlets with Marsala, 77
Chicken Cutlets with Pizza Sauce, 82
Chicken Cutlets with Prosciutto, 78
Chicken Cutlets with White Wine, 88
Chicken Legs with Porcini and Marsala, 85
Chicken Parmesan Clelia Style, 75
Chicken Piccata, 74
Chicken Thighs alla Clelia, 91
Chicken Thighs with Mushrooms and Cognac, 79
Chicken with Ginger, 83
Chicken with Gorgonzola Sauce, 81
Chickpea Salad, 25
Clelia's Classic Lasagna, 54
Clelia's Antipasto, 10
Clelia's Cannoli, 162
Clelia's Easter Roasted Lamb, 109
Clelia's Meatballs, 99
Cod in White Wine and Lemon, 131
Cod with Marinated Artichokes, 116
Cod with Puttanesca Sauce, 124
Cod with Three Peppers, 115
Cold Barley Salad, 27

Eggplant Boats, 136
Eggplant Cutlets, 146
Eggplant Parmesan Neapolitan Style, 138
Escarole and Cannellini Beans, 70
Escarole and Little Meatballs, 69
Fennel with Blood Oranges, 26
Fettuccine Alfredo Clelia Style, 64
Fresh Tuna Balls over Spaghetti, 119
Fresh Tuna Steaks Clelia Style, 130
Fresh Tuna with Herbs and Tomatoes, 121
Frisee Salad, 23

Green Beans with Cannellini, 145
Green Beans with Rosemary, 144
Halibut with Prosciutto, 117
Italian Dessert Pizza, 164
Italian Vegetable Casserole, 140

Lemon Sole with Breadcrumbs and Lemon, 132

Lentil Soup with Sausage, 68
Linguini with Parmesan and Provolone Cubes, 60
Neapolitan Potato Pie, 160
Nectarines or Peaches in Wine, 173
Nectarines with Amaretto and Pecans, 172
Orange and Arugula Salad, 28
Orzo Pasta with Asparagus, 46

Pappardelle with Bolognese Sauce, 30
Pasta and Bean Soup, 66
Pasta Carbonara, 33
Pasta Puttanesca, 59
Pasta with Salted Ricotta, 37
Pasta with Shellfish in a Gorgonzola Sauce, 44
Penne with Red and Yellow Peppers, 34
Peppers and Prosciutto Rollups, 11
Pine Nut Cookies, 165
Polenta Panini, 14
Pork Chops with Fennel Sauce, 108
Pork Chops with Olives and Pine Nuts, 112

Ravioli in a Butter and Sage Sauce, 62
Ricotta Cream Pie, 167
Ricotta Pie with Gran Gala Liqueur, 168
Roasted Tomatoes with Mozzarella, 153
Roasted Tricolor Peppers Rollups, 8
Rotini with Chicken, Asparagus, and Sour Cream, 42
Rotini with Fresh Vegtables and Goat Cheese, 45
Rotini with Pesto Mediterraneo, 31

Salmon with Pignoli Nuts, 114
Scallops with Rosemary, 123
Shells with Broccoli Rabe and Sausage, 56
Shells with Ricotta and Mozzarella, 38
Shrimp Scampi, 127
Shrimp with Peppers and Polenta Wedges, 128
Simple Fennel Salad, 21
Smoked Salmon and Artichoke Hearts Platter, 16
Spaghetti with Garlic and Oil, 39
Spaghetti with Pesto Genovese, 51
Spicy Artichoke Hearts, 155
Spinach Salad with Roasted Pecans, 20
Steak Pizzaiola, 95
Strufoli, 171
Stuffed Pizzelle, 174
Stuffed Apples, 170
Stuffed Artichokes, 148
Stuffed Bread with Sausage or Peppers, 12
Stuffed Chicken Thighs, 87
Stuffed Eggplant Rollups, 151
Stuffed Filet of Sole, 125
Stuffed Fresh Sardines, 133
Stuffed Peppers, 156
Stuffed Pork Tenderloin, 106
Stuffed Shells, 40
Stuffed Turkey Breast, 92
Stuffed Veal Chops, 104

Tiramisu' Clelia Style, 166
Tomatoes, Basil, and Mozzarella Salad, 24
Veal Chops with Cognac and Peppercorns, 101
Veal Cutlets alla Clelia, 102

Vegetable Lasagna, 52
Warm Spinach Salad with Goat Cheese, 22
Ziti with Herbs and Gorgonzola, 36
Ziti with Mushrooms and Artichokes, 58
Zucchini Soup, 72

Made in the USA
Charleston, SC
03 March 2017